There are few feelings more gut-wrenching than the feeling of hopelessness. It can feel like digging yourself out of a deep hole that never ends. And so many times, the Lord puts us there so we can find ourselves more completely dependent on Him than we ever thought we could be. I'm so thankful for my pastor, Adam Dooley, and the testimony to God's faithfulness through his son Carson's cancer journey. His testimony of faith builds up my faith, and I know it will build up yours too.

TRAVIS COTTRELL, singer/songwriter,
worship pastor at Englewood Baptist Church

Adam Dooley's writing exquisitely combines a pastor's heart and a theologian's insight with the anguished cries of a grieving parent. Offering no easy or glib answers, this story tore at my heart and then filled it with praise. It eloquently conducted me through a child's hospital room and into an empty tomb in Jerusalem. What a word of hope and reassurance for suffering Christians who cannot understand why God has allowed their pain.

HERSHAEL YORK, dean of the School of Theology,
Victor and Louise Lester Professor of Christian Preaching,
The Southern Baptist Theological Seminary

Adam and Heather Dooley are dear friends to my wife, Charlotte, and me. They are also heroes. Watching them walk through child leukemia with their son Carson deeply moved and inspired us. You will find a snippet of their family's story in this powerful little book. It is brutally honest, but it is also filled with encouragement and wisdom. If you're going through a tough time at this moment, I heartily recommend this book. It may have a word from our Lord that is just for you.

DANIEL L. AKIN, president,
Southeastern Baptist Theological Seminary

Adam Dooley felt his life was unraveling in one day with the shocking news that his three-year-old son had been diagnosed with leukemia. In *Hope When Life Unravels*, Adam shares openly and honestly of the gut-wrenching struggle his family faced for the next three years and how the Lord carried them through in a very powerful way. This book will be so helpful to anyone facing a time of suffering—not only with Adam's honest account of his personal journey but also with his rich biblical and theological insight on how God strengthened him and his family in this challenging time. I recommend this book for anyone—and especially as a gift to someone you know who feels that life is unraveling.

BRYANT WRIGHT, senior pastor,
Johnson Ferry Baptist Church, Marietta, Georgia

Life is fragile, and the threads of our existence can come unraveled at any moment in unexpected, cruel, devastating ways. My great friend Adam Dooley has written a heartrending but soul-blessing book on how to navigate the stormy seas of life when the waves are so high and the winds are so strong that only God can steer you safely home. For the hurting, the hopeless, and the helpless, Dr. Dooley's book is a must-read and a life preserver for those who feel as if they are going under for the last time.

JAMES MERRITT, senior pastor,
Cross Pointe Church, Duluth, Georgia

The greatest teacher in life is suffering, and there's no better person to speak on this topic than someone who has endured the trials of suffering himself. Speaking from his own personal experience, Adam Dooley gives us a biblical theology, coupled with practical experiences, on how to respond to life's most difficult trials. You're going to be challenged and encouraged to face whatever situation life presents.

ROBBY GALLATY, senior pastor,
Long Hollow Baptist Church, Hendersonville, Tennessee,
and author of *The Forgotten Jesus* and *Here and Now*

Adam and his family share an intensely personal struggle that is universal to all of us. Suffering, loss, or difficulties of life may remain unexplainable, but God stays constant. In this book, real-life experiences are undergirded by scriptural references to give us hope when all seems hopeless. Read this book to have your faith increased.

JIM RICHARDS, executive director,
Southern Baptists of Texas Convention

As has been proved true many times, we are all either in a storm, headed for a storm, or coming out of a storm. There are usually many questions, accompanied by a roller coaster of emotions. *Hope When Life Unravels* is a deeply personal but strongly biblical message of comfort to God's people. It will inspire you to run *to* God in times of trial, not *from* Him. I have been encouraged, challenged, and blessed by reading it, and I know you will be too.

DR. BRUCE FRANK, lead pastor,
Biltmore Church, Arden, North Carolina

As parents, we would rather endure any kind of pain and hardship than see our child walk through them. When those trials come, we face a choice: turn away from God out of resentment or draw nearer to Him, despite our inability to fully understand. I'm grateful for Adam's account of his family's journey through the excruciating battle of childhood cancer. His candor and transparency draw us deeply into this story, and the lessons he draws give us a reassurance that even in the darkest storm, the anchor indeed holds strong.

KEVIN EZELL, president,
North American Mission Board, SBC

HOPE WHEN LIFE UNRAVELS

Finding God When It Hurts

ADAM B. DOOLEY

ZONDERVAN
BOOKS

ZONDERVAN BOOKS

Hope When Life Unravels
Copyright © 2020 by Adam B. Dooley

Requests for information should be addressed to:
Zondervan, *3900 Sparks Dr. SE, Grand Rapids, Michigan 49546*

Zondervan titles may be purchased in bulk for educational, business, fundraising, or sales promotional use. For information, please email SpecialMarkets@Zondervan.com.

ISBN 978-0-310-35929-6 (audio)

Library of Congress Cataloging-in-Publication Data

Names: Dooley, Adam B., 1977- author.
Title: Hope when life unravels : finding God when it hurts / Adam B. Dooley.
Description: Grand Rapids : Zondervan, 2020. | Summary: "This is the next best
    book about why God doesn't answer our prayers when bad things happen. Dr.
    Adam Dooley searches for answers about God and human suffering. Why does
    God allow suffering? Dooley shares rich insights about the nature of God against
    the backdrop of his son's story, who was diagnosed with leukemia at age three"—
    Provided by publisher.
Identifiers: LCCN 2019050489 (print) | LCCN 2019050490 (ebook) | ISBN
    9780310359272 (trade paperback) | ISBN 9780310359289 (ebook)
Subjects: LCSH: Suffering--Religious aspects--Christianity. | Critically ill children.
Classification: LCC BT732.7 .D66 2020 (print) | LCC BT732.7 (ebook) | DDC
    248.8/6—dc23
LC record available at https://lccn.loc.gov/2019050489
LC ebook record available at https://lccn.loc.gov/2019050490

Cover design: Spencer Fuller / Faceout Studio
Interior design: Kait Lamphere
Interior images: All images courtesy of the Dooley family, unless otherwise noted.

Printed in the United States of America

20 21 22 23 24 25 26 27 28 29 /LSC/ 15 14 13 12 11 10 9 8 7 6 5 4 3 2 1

To my precious son—
I love you with all my heart.
Your life has been a crucible
of sanctification for me.

CONTENTS

INTRODUCTION

I still remember the musty smell of the room. Cartoon characters decorated wood-paneled walls, and stacks of children's books sat on both sides of our chairs. I knew that whatever the doctor was about to share couldn't be good. The events of the previous week seemed to point to it, and the mood of the office personnel only confirmed that this was not a typical test result. Nestled between my legs with his arms around my waist, my three-year-old son, Carson, seemed oblivious to what was happening. And why wouldn't he be? Like any carefree child, this superhero-wannabe's only concern was how long we would have to stay in the doctor's office.

I tried to reassure myself that I was probably overreacting. The swollen lymph nodes on Carson's head, behind his ears, and under his arms were concerning, but his blood tests last month didn't indicate any reason for alarm. Following a visit to family in Kentucky the previous week, it did seem strange that Carson lacked his usual energy, but most likely it was a nagging virus that wouldn't go away. More puzzling, however, was the bright red rash that stretched from under his chin to the top of his chest and was smooth to the touch. That was what prompted a Sunday afternoon checkup in the first place. Convinced that something more serious was wrong, my wife, Heather, insisted that waiting until Monday morning wasn't an option. As it turns out, she was right.

After seeing the rash, our pediatrician, Dr. Roberts, ordered more blood work. Meanwhile, I was preaching the morning worship service at our church. A text message from Heather was waiting when I walked into my office. She explained what was happening and asked that I come to the hospital as quickly as I could. I arrived just after the doctor encouraged us to grab a bite of lunch while we waited for the lab results. Eating was difficult due to our nerves, but Carson and our one-year-old, Brady, were ready for a break. Shortly after our meal, the phone rang, and a nurse asked us to return to the doctor's office, but she refused to share any information over the telephone. This only heightened the anxiety, making a ten-minute drive feel like an eternity. When that same nurse met us at the door and asked if she could watch our kids while we spoke with the doctor, every internal alarm went off. What were we walking into? Despite our apprehension, nothing could have prepared us for what came next.

When Dr. Roberts walked in the room and sat on the round stool in front of us, both her posture and facial expression communicated concern. "I wish I had better news," she said, "but I believe that Carson has leukemia." *Leukemia? Not Carson! How is that possible?* I knew little about pediatric cancer at this point, and my knowledge about cancer in general was frightening. Immediately, my heart began pounding, and tears quickly followed. By now Heather was breaking down beside me. Carson, who refused to stay with the nurse, watched this scene unfold and began comforting each of us. Obviously, a three-year-old doesn't understand words like *leukemia*. His tender little heart, however, was breaking—not for himself but for his parents.

"Please don't cry, Mommy!" he pleaded. "Everything is going to be okay, Daddy! I promise." These words were comforting reminders of why we loved him so much and desperate warnings of how deeply we were afraid of losing him.

What came next was a whirlwind of activity that set into motion a journey that continues today. We held each other, wept, prayed, and wept some more. Our godly doctor prayed with us and then gave us time alone to process. As we tried to regain our composure, Heather and I agreed that our extended family needed to know. The first phone call I made, however, was to a trusted mentor and friend who is both a moral compass and wind of strength in my life. He listened quietly and then prayed for us through his tears. Somewhere in his words, the Spirit of God revived my sense of responsibility and purpose in caring for my family. Despite my personal anxieties, I knew God wanted to use me in their lives at this moment. Soon I was calling our immediate family to break the news. The calls took on a pattern of horrified silence followed by tears. By this time, a colleague and friend was standing at the end of the hall in the tiny office complex. Nearly thirty years prior, he and his wife lost a child to cancer, and his presence was reassuring to me.

Though time seemed to stand still, a second blow jolted us back into reality. "Carson must be admitted to the hospital tonight," Dr. Roberts explained. Her words were direct but not cold. "You have two options going forward. He can be treated here in Mobile or at St. Jude Children's Research Hospital in Memphis, Tennessee."

"What would you recommend?" I asked.

"There are advantages to both," she said, "and the success rates here are almost as good as they are in Memphis."

Almost. Such a small word, but it made a monumental difference. How many of you reading this book realize that when you are talking about your babies, your most precious worldly possession, *almost* just isn't good enough? The decision was made.

By 5:00 p.m. we got in our car and drove home in a daze. Having recently moved to Mobile in order to pastor a new congregation, I had no idea how long it would take to drive to Memphis and wondered when we would arrive. Soon my phone rang, and I heard a reassuring voice on the other end of the line. "Pastor, I know what's happening, and I want to help. Please don't drive to Memphis. Let me fly you there in my plane. I'm making preparations. Just be at the airport as soon as you can." Gratitude and disbelief overwhelmed me. Though I was thankful for this sacrificial act of generosity, I simply could not believe any of it was happening. *Why us? Why now? Why this?* Feelings of anger, frustration, and bewilderment ravaged my mind. There was little time, however, to camp out on the highway of disbelief. We made our way home and threw clothes into our suitcases before driving to the airport.

As fear welled up in my heart, myriad questions bombarded me. Can we handle this? Is our faith strong enough? Will we lose our little boy? Why is this happening?

As we ascended off the runway, I looked out at the lights of this unfamiliar city we were trying to make home. In my heart I knew that things would never be the same. Two hours later, we landed safely in Memphis, jumped into a rental car, and drove to St. Jude Hospital. By 10:00 p.m. Carson was in a bed and nurses began checking vitals and running more tests. These events seemed like a nightmare, but I wasn't waking up. Our near-perfect, neatly packaged Christian life was unraveling. As fear welled up in my heart, myriad questions bombarded me. *Can we handle this? Is our faith strong enough? Will we lose our little boy? Why is this happening at all? Of all the people forced to go through a trial like this, why did God choose us?*

NOT A BOOK ABOUT CANCER

All of us have at least one thing in common. We are in a storm, headed for a storm, or coming out of a storm. I've heard those words from countless Bible teachers and felt compelled to share them with the congregation I led on what began as a typical Sunday morning. Little did I know that my family was about to live out the reality I was sharing with our church family that day. In just a few hours, the trajectory of our lives changed forever, and everything I believed and taught others would be put to the ultimate test. For the first time, quick solutions and trite explanations would not comfort the deep trouble of my soul. That's why I've written this book. Though every trial is different, suffering is painful, and no one is immune. We all hurt deeply at certain points of life (some more than others), and when those moments unfold, trivial slogans and popular action plans simply will not comfort a wilting spirit.

So this is not a book about cancer. Yes, I will share the powerful story of our son, who battled leukemia heroically. And yes, the lessons God taught us over a strenuous three-year period will be chronicled here. But my main purpose is to comfort others with the comfort I received from the Lord (2 Corinthians 1:4–5). Your adversity may be different, but don't make the mistake of assuming that it isn't important or that it lacks benefit. The Bible has much to teach us about suffering, no matter what our particular circumstance is. My prayer is that God will use what He taught my family when storms blow into our lives. Despite the differences in what we face, the universal principles of Scripture are a healing balm for our greatest heartaches.

In addition, I hope to shatter what I believe are damaging myths about suffering that are being propagated by a prosperity gospel that is an insult to the purposes of God and the pain we often feel. These weak theologies emphasize receiving from God rather than resting in Him. Even worse, they diminish the rich treasures of growth and maturity that often accompany our deepest wounds. As a result, many feel alienated from God and angry over what He allows. Confusion abounds when tragedy strikes, as if God is surprised and impotent or, even worse, vindictive and cruel. My desire is that this book will bring hope to those who did not receive the answers they prayed for. Though the tapestry of God's sovereignty cannot be reduced by our simplicity, the Bible speaks with pointed clarity about the divine designs that accompany our worst days. Understanding some of these intentions emboldens us to trust God when His work is mysterious beyond our comprehension. Daring to believe that when God seems most absent, He is often most active has been a lifeline for me. I want the same for you.

Each chapter will share part of Carson's dramatic journey, followed by a biblical principle or application. While I pray you will be inspired by the activity of God in the lives of our family, my greatest hope is that you will be strengthened and renewed by His Word. I certainly don't have an answer for everything God does, but I have learned to trust Him anyway. May the same be true in your life!

DISCUSSION QUESTIONS

1. What is the worst news you have ever received? How did you handle it?
2. Has any particular circumstance or trial compelled you to pick up this book?
3. Do any of your questions about suffering hinder your relationship with God?

ONE

WHO'S REALLY TO BLAME FOR OUR SUFFERING?

W*hy is this happening?* Those words kept running through my head as what felt like the longest day of our lives continued to unfold. "He will need to be admitted to the hospital tonight, but we need to make sure he can travel first," explained our pediatrician. "His white blood count is dangerously high, and I'm not sure he can make the trip. We need to do more blood work before I release you," she said. Within a few hours the results came back, and Carson was cleared for the journey to Memphis. After parting with our one-year-old son, Brady, for the first time, we boarded a small plane donated by a friend in order to travel to a place we knew little about. Carson was excited to fly in an aircraft that required him to wear headphones. He seemed so carefree and looked so healthy. The question *Why is God doing this?* continued to attack every thought.

After arriving in Memphis, none of us said a word as we listened to the GPS in our rental car direct us through each turn. My solitary despair gave way to anger the closer we got to St. Jude Children's Research Hospital. Don't get me wrong,

I was thankful for a place dedicated to curing pediatric cancer but angry that we needed to be there. As we checked in for the first time, my cynicism morphed into anger. *Why us? Why now? Why this? Why Carson? Why? Why? Why?*

First trip to Memphis on a friend's plane

The need to discern the reason behind our pain is a common reaction to trials. Perhaps it was a failed marriage, an unsuccessful surgery, a shattered dream, or a broken promise. For you it may be an addiction that won't leave you alone, a wrong decision that still haunts you, or a burden that is too great to talk about. Whatever form it takes, the looming question on the horizon of your heart is, "Why?" *Why did God allow this? Why won't God give me a miracle? Why does this hurt so badly? Why won't God help me?*

Why am I confined to a wheelchair?
Why are my children rebelling?
Why don't I ever get any breaks?
Why does life have to be so hard?

Why? Why? Why? Moments like these are pivotal because they leave us angry with God or more reliant on Him. Closer examination also reveals that the root of this question is much deeper than a need for answers. Our quest for explanations is often driven by our need for assurance that God still cares and that He hasn't deserted us, despite what we face in life. Even more, general inquiries are driven by the same hunger for reassurance that God has not forgotten or turned against the human race. *Why do so many people suffer in the world? Why is there sickness and pain? Why is the globe ravaged by tsunamis, hurricanes, tornadoes, and storms?*

PERMISSION TO ASK

Before attempting to answer the why behind the painful realities of suffering, we should first acknowledge that asking the question is permissible when we are hurting and confused. Occasionally, well-meaning Christians or Bible teachers will either explicitly or implicitly caution that asking God why is out of bounds. For some, it is an insult to the wisdom of God. For others, it demonstrates a tremendous lack of faith. And for many, humility and questions cannot coexist. As a pastor, I often stand by the bedside of sick church members, only to hear a family member retort, "I know we aren't supposed to ask God why . . ." Though such assertions appear to take the moral high road, they often leave sincere believers battling guilt over their questions or, even worse, denying that their questions exist at all.

Thankfully, the Bible nowhere teaches that it is sinful to ask God why. Outside of Jesus Christ, no single person suffered more than the Old Testament character Job. Recorded in a book that bears his name, the story of this remarkable man recounts the raw, burdensome realities that often accompany life's struggles. Over the course of his suffering, Job cried, "Why?" to the Lord twenty different times.

- Why do You contend with me? (10:2)
- Why did You bring me out of the womb? (10:18)
- Why do You hide Your face and consider me Your enemy? (13:24)

On one occasion, Job even uses the image of a courtroom and expresses his desire to argue his case before God. Yet despite all of his questions, when the book concludes, Job is never rebuked or corrected for asking why. Because his inquiries did not impugn the character of God, they become a good model for us to follow.

Additionally, Moses asked God why He sent him to lead the nation of Israel (Exodus 5:22), Joshua asked God why He was allowing Israel to be destroyed (Joshua 7:7), and the prophets Isaiah and Jeremiah asked God why He dealt so harshly with Israel (Isaiah 63:17; Jeremiah 14:19). Perhaps most stunning of all, however, is the remarkable lament of Jesus on the cross when He cried out, "My God, My God, why have You forsaken Me?" (Matthew 27:46).

In none of these instances will you find God irritated or angry because of the question. The greatest Christians in history, even the Son of God Himself, battled dark moments that compelled them to ask God why He was doing certain things in their lives. At times the answer comes; in other instances the questions remain. Despite Job's repeated inquiry of the Lord, there is no indication he ever understood the reason behind his suffering. Asking God why bad things happen is always permissible, but demanding that He answer is not.

WHY SO MUCH SUFFERING?

The origin of suffering is as old as the first man (Adam) and woman (Eve). Repeatedly throughout the Genesis narrative of creation, God declared all that He made to be good. The light was good (1:4); the earth and seas were good (1:10); the vegetation was good (1:12); the sea creatures and birds were good (1:21); the beasts of the earth were good (1:25). Then God made man in His own image to rule over His creation, which He declared good in its entirety (1:26–31). After putting Adam and Eve in the Garden of Eden, God gave just one restriction regarding their behavior. Genesis 2:16–17 reads, "The LORD God commanded the man, saying, 'From any tree of the garden you may eat freely; but from the tree of the knowledge of good and evil you shall not eat, for in the day that you eat from it you will surely die.'" Though hard for us to imagine, there was no death, no sickness, no natural disaster, and no suffering of any kind. Throughout the cosmos, every part of God's creation functioned exactly as it was designed to. Peace, health, safety, and contentment were the rule rather than the exception.

Then everything changed when Adam and Eve succumbed to the first temptation. Disguised as a serpent, Satan persuaded the first couple to partake from the one tree God forbade. Believing they would become like God, Adam and Eve birthed sin into the entire human race with all of its consequences (Genesis 3:1–6).

Romans 5:12 offers this commentary: "Through one man sin entered into the world, and death through sin, and so death spread to all men, because all sinned." Because of Adam's sin, all people are born sinners, and all sinners will die. Though not immediately, God warns that the couple will return to the dust of the earth (Genesis 3:19). Likewise, subsequent generations have met the same fate because of their/our inherited depravity. A cursory reading of Genesis genealogies reveals that the average life span of individuals declined in light of sin's presence. Quality of life declined as each decade introduced more severe evidences of human fallenness. Disease, sickness, war, strained relationships, and rampant selfishness characterize the condition of everyone born of an earthly father and mother.

These consequences touched more than the human race, however, for God's perfect creation was also marred as a casualty to sin. In what is often called the curse, God immediately pronounced the far-reaching impact of disobedience (Genesis 3:16–19). Romans 8 elaborates on this theme by personifying creation as an anxious onlooker awaiting the redemption of human beings (Romans 8:19). Why does this matter? Better still, why should we care?

Romans 8:20–21 explains, "For the creation was subjected to futility, not willingly, but because of Him who subjected it, in hope that the creation itself also will be set free from its slavery to corruption into the freedom of the glory of the children of God." The idea is that no part of creation works properly. Rain waters the earth, but it also causes flooding. Winds provide a gentle relaxing breeze, but they also cause hurricanes and tornadoes. The earth produces much beautiful vegetation, but it also bears weeds and thorns. Scorching heat, blistering cold, natural disasters, and the nature of animals are but a few examples of creation's deviation from God's original design. No part of God's handiwork is untouched by the enslaving corruption of sinfulness, and the entire cosmos waits to be set free from the curse of depravity. Romans 8:22 laments, "We know that the whole creation groans and suffers the pains of childbirth together until now."

THE VIEW FROM THE GROUND

Understanding these generalities may not be difficult, but living in light of them proves to be more challenging. Every heartache, burden, trial, and unwelcome circumstance in your life is either directly or indirectly caused by sin. At times, sinful choices bring certain consequences. Personal sin can wreak havoc in your life, causing untold sorrows. Disobedience to God causes trouble and pain wherever it is found. Sometimes we suffer, and we can only blame ourselves because we are directly responsible. Even then, our spiritual parents from the Garden of Eden stand in the shadows as abetting accomplices. Because we are sinful descendants of Adam and Eve, our nature compels us to rebel—and we hurt as a result.

Not all suffering, however, is the result of personal sin. While sin causes all suffering generally, this does not mean that *your* sin is always the particular cause. Much of the pain we must endure is an indirect by-product of wickedness in general. Maybe you were hurt by the actions of others, such as a spouse, coworker, friend, or stranger. At other times your trauma might be "accidental" in the sense that the fallenness of creation rather than an individual is to blame. Sickness, natural disasters, and painful circumstances can fall in this category. We often groan with the

25

rest of creation, knowing that apart from God's intervention, the calamities of life will continue (Romans 8:23).

Unfortunately, the emotional gravity of our tragedy and pain sometimes overshadows these eternal truths. Blaming God for our circumstances will leave us empty and hopeless, yet this is often our temptation. Though we seldom praise Him for what He prevents, God is often scolded for what He allows. We tend to be slow with our gratitude for happiness and quick with our contempt when things don't unfold according to plan. This, too, points to the damning consequences of sin in our lives.

God is not to blame for your suffering.
*He is **not** your enemy;*
He is your only hope!

But why should I chastise God when I am hurting? The first week after Carson's diagnosis was the most difficult of his entire treatment for me. Filled with anger, fear, anxiety, and questions, I found it difficult to talk to God. Despite what I knew in my head, the pull of my heart desired to blame someone for my son's predicament. Sensing my folly, I read Genesis 3 in earnest. Then on a piece of paper, I wrote the words, "Leukemia is a consequence of the Fall. I will not chastise God for it. He is my only hope." That moment of clarity anchored my heart to a simple truth that can change one's outlook forever: *God is not to blame for your suffering.* He is *not* your enemy; He is your only hope!

HOPE YOU CANNOT LIVE WITHOUT

Understanding where suffering originates frees us to seek God for refuge rather than approach Him with our inquisitive demands and frustrations. But what hope does God provide us? Even if God is not the source of our earthly pain, what can He do about it? Returning to Genesis 3 and Paul's explanatory comments in Romans 8 will help us answer these plaguing questions. We have hope in God despite our circumstances.

First, God can save us from the direct and indirect consequences of sin. God promised Eve that the seed of the woman would ultimately crush the head of the serpent (Genesis 3:15). As the first prophetic word about a coming Messiah, this verse encourages us that God will not leave us to endure the consequences of our actions eternally. Because women do not possess a seed for producing a child, this promise points to the virgin conception of Jesus Christ wrought by the Holy Spirit. Later called the second Adam or the last Adam (Romans 5:12–21; 1 Corinthians 15:45–49), Jesus came to rescue those who call out to Him despite their sins. Though we still live in fallen flesh (Romans 7:13; 8:1) and in a depraved world full of suffering (1 John 5:19), through God's promised Messiah our sins can be forgiven and our home in heaven can be secured.

In this sense, all suffering is temporary when measured against the backdrop of eternity (Romans 8:18). Despite our earthly pain, Scripture promises that our "momentary, light affliction is producing for us an eternal weight of glory far beyond all comparison, while we look not at the things which are seen, but at the things which are not seen; for the things which are seen are temporal, but the things which are not seen are eternal" (2 Corinthians 4:17–18).

Added to these reassurances, God controls your suffering, even though He did not cause it. Key to our understanding that good can come out of our trials is the ability of God to work through those circumstances for different purposes. Satan, for example, was directly responsible for the calamity Job faced, but God used it for outcomes all His own. How else can we explain that God gave permission for every level of assault hurled at Job (Job 1:12; 2:6)?

If God is unable to control the timing, degree, and duration of our trials, any notion of drawing strength from His purpose and design is mythical. Yet the God of the Bible is not only aware of earthly dilemmas; He meticulously places them for reasons beyond our comprehension. Though this forces us to follow a God we don't always understand, the alternative is a God who is unable to provide any substantive hope in our troubles because He is just as surprised by them as we are.

By contrast, Romans 8:20 says that God "subjected" creation to "futility," or the consequences and curse of sin, but He did so "in hope." In other words, God uses the course of sin to bring about the redemption of the physical universe and believers through the person of Jesus Christ. God the Father controlled every consequence of sin to bring about the death and resurrection of His Son in order to set us free from our prison of pain and death. He still uses suffering today (and we'll discuss this in a later chapter), but God remains powerful and trustworthy in our deepest sorrows. The apostle Peter captures the essence of the principle: "Therefore, those also who suffer according to the will of God shall entrust their souls to a faithful Creator in doing what is right" (1 Peter 4:19).

The Lord also uses our suffering for a greater good. Whether we personally benefit or others are beneficiaries of our traumatic outcomes, God is always working behind the scenes of calamity to bring purpose to each difficulty that plagues us. Romans 8:28

reassures us that we can be certain "God causes all things to work together for good to those who love God, to those who are called according to His purpose."

The Old Testament story of Joseph brings the principle to life. As the youngest of twelve brothers, Joseph was the spoiled favorite who loved to serve his father as a tattletale (Genesis 37:2). The more his father loved him, the more his brothers hated him. This favoritism, however, in no way justifies the harsh brutality shown toward young Joseph by his siblings. They plot to kill him, assault him, sell him into slavery, and then deceive their father Jacob about the whole matter (Genesis 37:18–32). From a human perspective, Joseph's life is ruined beyond repair. But unbeknownst to Joseph, God is working to save Israel from a coming drought and to fulfill an earlier promise made to Abraham (Genesis 15:13–14).

Toward the end of his life, Joseph confronts his brothers without malice or regret: "As for you, you meant evil against me, but God meant it for good in order to bring about this present result, to preserve many people alive" (Genesis 50:20). The life-long suffering and sacrifice of one man resulted in the salvation of Israel. Broaden the horizon of redemptive history a bit more, and you'll discover that God was also providentially preparing the way for a Messiah who died for the whole world. No Israel, no Jesus. No Jesus, no salvation. No salvation, no hope. You and I stand as direct beneficiaries of the good that God brought out of Joseph's trials!

The results will be different when we suffer today, but the principle remains the same. Sometimes the privilege of hindsight will reveal how you are personally reaping the beneficial harvest that flows out of enduring difficult seasons in your life.

Other times, the practical impact that your troubles is having on others will bring you satisfaction. When these realities aren't apparent, however, eternity will reveal the fruit of your sacrifice. Like Joseph, you might look over the span of history from the peace of eternity and discover that your life touched countless people you never lived to meet. No matter how God reveals your victories, choose to believe in the meantime that He can and will bring good out of your suffering.

DISCUSSION QUESTIONS

1. What is it about the author's reflections in this chapter that resonates with you most?
2. Do you feel guilty when you question God's activity in your life?
3. What is the ultimate cause of all the pain that is in the world today?
4. Why is walking through trials so difficult, even though we can grasp their origin?
5. Where can you find hope when you are hurting the worst?

TWO THE DARK SIDE OF GOD'S LOVE

Just ten minutes into hearing the doctor's explanations, I could take it no longer. We were already numb from the events of the day, but hearing Carson scream in the background pushed me over the edge. While I was signing waivers just outside his newly inhabited hospital room, nurses on the second floor of St. Jude began the painful process of drawing blood for initial testing, sending Carson into a panic unlike anything before or since. Despite the frustration of the young doctor needing to follow his protocol, I turned my back to him and darted into the tiny room. On the bed in front of me, four nurses were nearly prostrate as they tried to hold each of Carson's limbs down. His screams were rivaled only by his newfound strength as he resisted the necessary IV needle. To the left of the bed, Heather was crying as I made my way to the opposite side. Unable to speak fluently because of his violent trembling, Carson shouted broken words to me as he gasped for air. "Make them stop, Daddy!" "Please take me home!" "Don't do this to me!"

Everything inside me wanted to pick him up in my arms and end this unwanted interruption of our lives. I fought back tears, knowing that retreat wasn't an option. Rubbing his arm for comfort, I tried to explain to Carson that the pain would only last a moment. Tears welled up in his big blue eyes, making it clear that I could not alleviate his anxieties. For the first time in his brief life, my son was unable to trust my protection. This realization was deeper than any needle for me. Reasoning with a three-year-old about something so traumatic, however, is an impossible battle to win. I knew what I had to do, and I knew Carson was not going to like it.

I stretched my body over his, grabbing both wrists, pinning him to the bed. Instinctively, Carson realized the force I exerted made me an accomplice to those in the room rather than the hero he so desperately wanted. The nurses moved quickly, recognizing their opportunity. Unfortunately, our positioning left us nose to nose and eye to eye. I pressed my forehead against his to offer reassurance. "This will only take a second, son," I whispered. The words didn't help. "No, Daddy! Don't do this! I can't take this! Get away from me! Leave me alone!"

Encouraging gifts lifted Carson's spirit that first week.

These words stung my heart even as the needles pierced Carson's arms. I felt tears dripping off the end of my nose and knew I had to pull it together. My only reassurance was that the one thing Carson least wanted was also the single thing he most needed at that moment. It was right for me to force him because

I knew better than he did what was best. *He will understand one day*, I thought, *that I'm only doing this because I love him so much.* Then in a moment of clarity it dawned on me: this is *exactly* what God does for me. Immediately, God spoke to my heart and said, "I love you more than you could ever love Carson. Will you trust Me to give you what you need instead of what you want? You need this trial too."

HARD PROVIDENCE

Providence is a word describing God's interaction with and supervision over the events of the world generally and people specifically. Simply put, God guides and directs every step we take according to His purposes and design. Understanding this reality raises questions about suffering, but it also provides great comfort when we discover the eternal benefits of our hardships. Admittedly, no one can understand the mind of God (Romans 11:33–36), and most of us earnestly ask God why when life begins to unravel. Often, our questions remain unanswered and our frustrations loom on the horizon as a weapon against faith in God.

Why did my spouse die?

Why did I lose my job?

Why is my family in disarray?

Why is my health declining?

Trusting God's providence, however, can liberate us from the nuisance of doubt and anxiety over what we do not understand. Realizing that God is working, even when we cannot fully comprehend how, enables us to face trials with the certainty of winning, regardless of the outcome. This requires confidence that God is trustworthy to give us what we need even when what we want is different. We can live knowing that though God's providence is sometimes hard, it is always good.

Consider the strange encouragement of Philippians 1:29: "For to you it has been granted for Christ's sake, not only to believe in Him, but also to suffer for His sake." Really? God "grants" us the opportunity to suffer for His sake? The idea is that we suffer not because we deserve it but because God graces us with the privilege. Perhaps we could live with the fact that He requires it, plans it, or even forces it on us. But who celebrates the notion that God grants us the improbable blessing of suffering? Why should we consider this a gracious invitation? After observing the weight that so many people carry, it seems insensitive and crude to hint that trials might be a privilege.

These words remind us that God allows Christians to represent Him to others through the witness that adversities provide. Even greater, however, is the indication that earthly difficulties are a unique means to know God better than we could otherwise. The apostle Paul spoke of his difficulties as a unique invitation to a deeper relationship with the Lord in Philippians 3:10: "that I may know Him and the power of His resurrection and the fellowship of His sufferings, being conformed to His death." While the power of Christ's resurrection is something all people desire in their lives, few are eager to embrace the fellowship of His suffering in order to know Him better. Yet experiencing the power of Christ's resurrection begins on the road of heartache. Don't forget that Jesus had to weather the agony of Golgotha before He reveled in the glory of an empty tomb. Likewise, a prerequisite to walking in the power of Jesus' resurrection is the willingness to have fellowship with Him through suffering. Thus, for Paul:

- everything gained is counted loss for Christ (Philippians 3:7).
- everything is loss compared to knowing Jesus personally (3:8).

The ultimate goal is "that I may attain to the resurrection from the dead" (Philippians 3:11). Far from casting doubt on Paul's confidence in the future res-urrection, these words highlight the resurrected reality that those who suffer for Christ enjoy. When we die to sin, selfishness, pettiness, dreams,

Experiencing the power of Christ's resurrection begins on the road of heartache.

aspirations, and goals, we are free to know Christ and live the resurrected life with Him today. Paul's progression teaches us that all of life's difficulties are:

- for the sake of Christ (Philippians 3:7).
- that I may gain Christ (3:8).
- that I may be found in Him (3:9).
- that I may know Him (3:10).

Furthermore, the old apostle concedes that:

- he hasn't already obtained this level of fellowship with Christ (3:12).
- he willingly forgets anything in the past that would hinder him (3:13).

- he reaches forward to what lies ahead in order to know Christ better (3:13–14).

The implications here are profound. God providentially allows hardships in our lives that are the opposite of what we desire because He knows they will meet our greatest need of knowing Him more intimately. Ironically, when God seems most distant because of what we face, He is often most active in our lives. When we least understand what God is doing, we are better positioned to know Him at a more personal level because of the faith we need to exercise. God's goal is not our comprehending Him more completely, but our trusting Him more deeply.

NO ONE IS IMMUNE

Those drawn to the suffering of Job typically possess both a reverence and fear as they approach the narrative because they are likely active participants in the story rather than casual observers. In reality, none of us know when the vital lessons found within its pages will be anchored into our lives. Yet, because all people hurt deeply at some point without explanation, the account of Job offers eternal insights to help us survive the worst of times.

For now, allow me to point out that Job's heartache came despite his integrity, not due to its absence. Job 1:1 reads, "There was a man in the land of Uz whose name was Job; and that man was blameless, upright, fearing God and turning away from evil." Here was a man who feared God and hated sin. He and his wife had a large family (seven sons and three daughters), and

Job was their spiritual leader (Job 1:2–5). The Bible makes it clear that despite being a sinner, Job wasn't afflicted as a result of any particular transgression. Despite our tendency to believe the opposite, righteous people sometimes suffer for no apparent reason. Though correction (1 Peter 4:15) and discipline (Hebrews 12:5–12) are realities for Christians who step out of fellowship with God, all trials are not a direct consequence of sinful actions. Certainly, in the case of Job, no act of disobedience warranted the degree of pain he faced.

Unfortunately, many religious charlatans teach just the opposite today. Religious empires are built on the false premise that walking in integrity and faith assures believers of lives free from sickness, heartache, or problems of any kind. Faith becomes a means of avoiding trials altogether rather than enduring them, as well as a gimmick to claim your reality from God. Among the heretical remains is a gospel of false assurance that promises unsuspecting followers what it cannot provide by turning God into the leader of an earthly kingdom. As with Job's deceived friends (Eliphaz, Bildad, and Zophar), there is little room for the notion that God uses suffering in the lives of the righteous just as He does in the lives of the unrighteous. Yet against this backdrop, the remarkable testimony of Job stands.

Furthermore, as the narrative unfolds, readers learn that Job is chosen to suffer not just *despite* his righteousness but *because* of it. Job 1:6–12 reads:

Now there was a day when the sons of God came to present themselves before the LORD, and Satan also came among them. The LORD said to Satan, "From where do you come?" Then Satan answered the LORD and said,

"From roaming about on the earth and walking around on it." The LORD said to Satan, "Have you considered My servant Job? For there is no one like him on the earth, a blameless and upright man, fearing God and turning away from evil." Then Satan answered the LORD, "Does Job fear God for nothing? Have You not made a hedge about him and his house and all that he has, on every side? You have blessed the work of his hands, and his possessions have increased in the land. But put forth Your hand now and touch all that he has; he will surely curse You to Your face." Then the LORD said to Satan, "Behold, all that he has is in your power, only do not put forth your hand on him." So Satan departed from the presence of the LORD.

Though I will deal with much of what is said here in a later chapter (see chapter 4), notice that Satan maintains that none on the earth are righteous. To counter, God allows the devil to wreak havoc in Job's life without physically hurting him. Consequently, Job loses all of his livestock, servants, and children in one fatal blow (Job 1:13–19). This doesn't sound like trouble-free living to me! None of us are immune to difficulties, sadness, and tragedy, even if we walk with God.

Job is chosen to suffer not just *despite* his righteousness but *because* of it.

Despite those who teach that suffering is the exception rather than the rule, the Bible clearly teaches that godly people suffer as much as others.

The book of Hebrews recounts the experiences of faithful believers who were mocked, scourged, imprisoned, stoned, sawn in two, and stabbed to death. Many of them hid in the desert, mountains, and caves, yet Scripture says these were those "of whom the world was not worthy" (Hebrews 11:36–39). Even more explicit is 1 Peter 2:21: "For you have been called for this purpose, since Christ also suffered for you, leaving you an example for you to follow in His steps." The integrity of these Christians is not diminished because they suffered; it is underscored. God is not powerless to prevent our afflictions; He is wise enough to plan them for our good! No amount of faith or integrity will protect us from hardship, because God actively pursues a deeper relationship with those who love Him.

HOW SHOULD WE RESPOND?

Please don't interpret my words as a celebration of the pain in people's lives. The tension arises because God clearly works through our adversities, yet they remain difficult nonetheless. Job's initial response to the calamity he faced is a worthy model for us to follow because it balances the trauma of the earthly with the perspective of the heavenly. Despite his desperation, bewilderment, and confusion, this wounded man responds by worshiping the Lord. Job 1:20–21 reads:

> Then Job arose and tore his robe and shaved his head, and he fell to the ground and worshiped. He said,

> "Naked I came from my mother's womb,
> And naked I shall return there.
> The Lord gave and the Lord has taken away.
> Blessed be the name of the Lord."

Note first that Job did not diminish the grief that was real in his life. Tearing his robe and shaving his head were outward signs of the internal calamity that shook Job to his core. Any idea that Christians should not grieve over their troubles falls short of biblical teaching. To the contrary, the only restriction is that believers should not grieve as those who have no hope (1 Thessalonians 4:13). Pretending that all is well when you are falling apart neither honors the Lord nor heals the soul. Stoic platitudes are nothing more than hypocritical masks that prevent us from reaping the full benefit of God's work in our lives.

No dichotomy exists between expressing genuine grief and expressing heartfelt worship. In fact, grief can drive us to worship, and worship can relieve our grief. Consider Jesus in Gethsemane just hours before the cross. Refusing to deny His anguish, He embraced it. Drops of blood fell from His brow as Jesus cried out to His Father and pleaded for another way to offer redemption. Yet throughout a night of intense prayer, the anchor to Jesus' pain was a resolved determination to worship the heavenly Father with unwavering obedience and praise.

> **God doesn't insist that we be happy because of our afflictions, but He does expect us to be hopeful about their outcome.**

God doesn't insist that we be happy because of our afflictions, but He does expect us to be hopeful about their outcome. Knowing that intimacy with God is the fruit of heartache and pain motivates us to endure every trial as a means to a greater good. Thus, we should worship God even when His purposes for us might not be clear. Like Job, we acknowledge that we are born with nothing and we die with nothing; therefore, everything God gives in between is a gift that He is entitled to take away. The money you lost was never yours anyway. The health that God took away was not your right or His obligation. The little boy I desperately feared losing does not belong to me.

Everything we love, cherish, and protect represents a blessing we did not merit or deserve. So if He gives, we worship Him. If He takes away, we worship Him still. The issue is not whether God is real, but whether God is enough during seasons of difficulty. He is all that we have and need on the day we are born and the day we die. Suffering reminds us that God is also everything we need to survive every day in between.

DISCUSSION QUESTIONS

1. Have you ever wanted something from God that contradicted what you needed?
2. Can you trust God even when He concludes that a trial will be beneficial for you?
3. What, if anything, should we conclude about others when they face hardship?
4. How can you acknowledge your struggles without diminishing your hope?

THREE

MORE THAN YOU CAN BEAR

The news that Carson needed a subcutaneous port on his chest almost pushed us over the edge. Since this device was necessary to avoid daily needle pokes, we later referred to it as Carson's buddy because of the pain it eliminated. Initially, however, this medical advancement was an unwelcome guest in my son's body. A stuffed doll with a Velcro patch just below the right shoulder showed us the incision's location and the port's placement. As we were already prepping for the reality that all his hair would soon fall out, the thought of surgically cutting Carson's perfectly smooth skin was more than we could take.

The end of our first full day in Memphis left each of us exhausted and frightened, wondering if the treatment plan would work and if Carson would live. Six weeks of intensive chemother apy lay before us, designed to propel his tiny body into remission. After this, St. Jude's protocol called for 128 consecutive weeks of treatment to prevent a relapse (which is very common for acute lymphoblastic leukemia patients). As I stared out the little red-framed window on the second floor of the hospital, I wondered how our family could make all this work. *Do we have what it takes? Is our faith strong enough?* Anxiety crept into my heart with

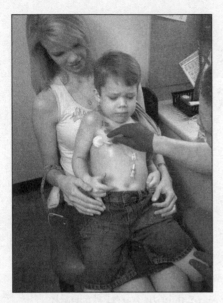
Accessing the port for the first time

greater force than I could bear. I felt as if I was about to break, wilting under the pressure of this unwanted circumstance.

Not knowing how to cope, I flipped open my laptop and found the website page created by a member of our church staff. CaringBridge.org gives families the opportunity to post updates and prayer requests regarding loved ones facing life-threatening illnesses. In addition, concerned family members and friends can post words of encouragement and strength. As I stared at the moonlight of Memphis for the second night in a row, I hoped this distraction would somehow preserve the sanity I feared I was losing. Already dozens of posts had filled the message board to assure our family of love and support. As I read each of them, I was grateful for such caring friends, but my anxieties grew with the realization that we needed these thoughts at all. I staggered between anger, frustration, and bewilderment—but mostly fear.

Then I read words that supernaturally arrested my attention. The message was simple, but the impact was profound. One line assured us that a young family in our church was praying for us— specifically that God would be glorified in our situation. It was the Scripture verse attached, however, that filled my heart with hope for the first time since leukemia ravaged our world. Taken from the text I preached just thirty-six hours prior, these words echoed in my heart like thunder from Mount Sinai. The verse was Matthew 7:25, which simply reads, "And the rain fell, and the floods came, and the winds blew and slammed against that house; and *yet* it did not fall, for it had been founded on the rock" (emphasis mine).

In that moment, it was as if God said to me, "You will not fall or break under this pressure. The rain is still falling, the flood will be fierce, and the wind will keep blowing, but your foundation is strong!" Tears rolled down my face as I thanked God for His strength. That hospital room turned into an altar where I gave my son and family to the Lord. As I watched Carson sleep, cuddled in the arms of his mother, I knew deep down we were going to survive this terrible storm.

A LIE YOU SHOULD REJECT

As I think back to what was the first of many potential breaking points during Carson's treatment, words of intended comfort and flippant words of counsel also fill my mind. Oftentimes, people simply don't know what to say when someone they care about is hurting. The compulsion to say something, however, leads many to offer trite explanations for deep problems and, even worse, unbiblical clichés that hinder rather than aid what God might be doing through the suffering we face. The one reckless comment I heard more than any other throughout our ordeal came from well-meaning people who wanted to lighten the load of what we were carrying. It usually surfaced when others could not fathom the duration required to treat Carson's cancer. It was almost predictable. "Remember, Pastor Adam, God won't ever put more on you than you can bear!"

Really? When I first heard those words, they made me angry. This certainly felt like much more than I could bear. Then, after hearing this statement repeatedly, I actually grieved for those who made it. Either these people never depended fully on the Lord or they somehow confused His strength for their own. God *often* puts more on us than we can bear, because He has every intention of bearing our burdens for us. Jesus said, "Come to Me, all who are weary and heavy-laden, and I will give you rest" (Matthew 11:28). How is it possible to know the rest of God without first being weary? How can you experience God as your burden bearer if you have no burdens to bear? Suffering reveals a side of Christ that we cannot know otherwise. Pulling ourselves up by our bootstraps is the opposite of the gospel that declares we can do nothing apart from Christ (John 15:5). So when others want to encourage you by reminding you how strong you are, don't believe it. It's a lie. Our weakness cannot sufficiently endure the complexities of a painful world where everything is tainted by sin.

This realization does not lead to our demise, however, for God is able and willing to carry every sorrow that overwhelms us and every trial that bewilders us. In fact, He promises:

But we have this treasure in earthen vessels, so that the surpassing greatness of the power will be of God and not from ourselves; we are afflicted in every way, but not crushed; perplexed, but not despairing; persecuted, but not forsaken; struck down, but not destroyed; always carrying about in the body the dying of Jesus, so that the life of Jesus also may be manifested in our body.

2 Corinthians 4:7–10

God allows us to be afflicted, perplexed, persecuted, and struck down in order to demonstrate His strength when we are not crushed, despairing, forsaken, or destroyed. The Holy Spirit bears, carries, shoulders, and endures what would understandably break us beyond repair.

When Paul faced an unnamed thorn in the flesh, he was desperate for God to remove it. Though he realized God's purpose was preserving his humility, the aged apostle beckoned the Lord three times to remove his affliction (2 Corinthians 12:7–8). Yet each time the Lord responded that His grace was sufficient and that His power is perfected in weakness (12:9). With God's intentions for him apparent, Paul contented himself to remain weak in order that the power of God might rest on him. He trusted God fully, knowing that His strength could consistently overcome any weakness caused by difficulty. Paul knew, as we should, that God unleashes His power on and through us when problems force our greater dependence on Him. Our comfort is not in believing that our troubles won't be great, but in celebrating that our God is much greater.

HOW DOES GOD BEAR OUR BURDENS?

If you dare believe my premise, practical questions remain. How does God bear our burdens? Where do we find relief when life unravels before our eyes? What are the means that God uses to become His hands and feet when we need Him the most?

The Body of Christ

The most obvious answer is people. Amazed by the body of Christ during his imprisonment, Paul wrote these words to believers in Philippi:

> I thank my God in all my remembrance of you, always offering prayer with joy in my every prayer for you all, in view of your participation in the gospel from the first day until now. For I am confident of this very thing, that He who began a good work in you will perfect it until the day of Christ Jesus. For it is only right for me to feel this way about you all, because I have you in my heart, since both in my imprisonment and in the defense and confirmation of the gospel, you all are partakers of grace with me.
>
> *Philippians 1:3–7*

Note his description of them as "partakers of grace." The grace he mentions is not saving grace, but strength to endure hardship for the sake of the gospel. Partaking of that grace bears the idea of fellowship for more than mutual enjoyment, but for the advancement of their Christian message instead. The commitment of the Philippians did not waver, even if it meant suffering alongside the beloved apostle. Supporting one another through difficult seasons undergirded the viability of the gospel that brought them together. No wonder Paul longed for these friends even as he prayed for them (Philippians 1:8).

God uses people in a similar way today. After Carson's initial prognosis, the overwhelming support of the Christian community around us lifted us up beyond our strength. The church I pastored at the time was somewhat formal in business matters, so they passed a resolution instructing me to stay with my family in Memphis until we could all return home together. Though that may sound like a needless formality, it was a touching demonstration of love and support within our mutual context. Because I had transitioned to a new pastorate just months before our battle with leukemia, the church I previously led in Chattanooga was equally supportive. These two congregations tangibly loved us from afar, even as Carson was receiving treatment in another city.

Added to this were countless birthday cards and gifts when Carson turned four years old just two weeks after his diagnosis. People began making donations to St. Jude in his honor. A charity fund was created to cover any of our incidental expenses. Thousands of messages appeared on a Caring Bridge website designed to keep friends abreast of Carson's condition. People all over the world committed to pray. When we began flying from Alabama to Memphis each week, the Delta Airlines team at the Pensacola Airport made every trip easier with their smiles, gifts, encouragement, and surprises. Many of these workers were professing Christians, and they became "partakers of grace" for us in order to lighten our load and strengthen our failing feet.

How is it possible for Christians to be so helpful when others are hurting? God allows His children to share the strength and comfort they received directly from Him. The Bible teaches that God "comforts us in all our affliction so that we will be able to comfort those who are in any affliction with the comfort with which we ourselves are comforted by God" (2 Corinthians 1:4). Every believer needs a community of other Christ-followers. Within the body of Christ, we find the collaborative strength to navigate painful experiences. When the Lord lifts the burdens of His children, He empowers them to do the same for others who suffer in similar ways. God uses fellow Christians who have already walked the same paths we face to bear some of the weight during our struggles. Scripture instructs believers to love one another (Romans 13:8), bear one another's burdens (Galatians 6:2), be kind to one another (Ephesians 4:32), comfort one another (1 Thessalonians 4:18), pray for one another (James 5:16), teach and admonish one another (Colossians 3:16), and serve one another (1 Peter 4:10).

Days at St. Jude were often long and tiring due to extended time in crowded waiting rooms filled with other children fighting the same offensive disease. With more than two years ahead of us, the beginning of our journey felt daunting in light of the responsible, busy lives that awaited us back home.

One particular morning brought a wave of emotions that left me discouraged beyond the daily struggle of our situation. Fighting back tears underneath my bowed head, I simply prayed for God to strengthen me for the moment. No sooner had I voiced those words in my head than I looked up to see a young father named Jason (whose son was also fighting leukemia) lean over to speak with me. Sensing my despair, he began to share the early days of their journey, which was just forty weeks from completion. Other parents shared similar stories, but I knew this father was different when he confessed, "I wasn't sure at first if I could continue pastoring while caring for my son."

Because I was feeling the same pressure and tension, those words struck a soothing chord in my soul. We then learned that our churches were just forty-five minutes apart. I listened intently as he shared about their weekly plane rides, time away from home, and managing a congregation with so much on his mind. His words were like a balm applied to the deepest fears in my heart regarding the future. Carson and I would later follow the same pattern each week as this father and son. My friendship with Jason remained a constant source of strength for me throughout the entirety of Carson's treatment. This initial conversation was one of the first moments when I actually felt a peace that my family would survive the horrible ordeal thrust on us. God was bearing my load through another brother who was further down the road than my experience at that point.

The Word of Christ

Added to the practical comfort God dispenses through His people are Scripture's revealed reassurances. Not only is the Bible the inspired Word of God without any errors, but it is also a sufficient source of guidance and strength when we are weathering the storms of life. A brief survey of the book of Psalms demonstrates the supernatural power and encouragement that come through the Scriptures when anxiety plagues us. Psalm 119, for example, reminds us that the Bible revives us (v. 25), strengthens us (v. 28), gives us hope (v. 49), comforts us (vv. 50, 52), protects us from evil (v. 101), gives us understanding (v. 104), sustains us (v. 116), gives us joy despite trouble (v. 143), and enables us to rejoice (v. 162).

Like a soft pillow inviting weary heads and hearts to find rest, these words remind us of the abiding, practical, and comforting work of God in our lives. Without the prophetic corrections of Scripture, the realities of a fallen world leave us wondering if there is any rhyme or reason to the hardships we face. Yet through the Bible, we learn how to respond to trials (James 1:2–4), that God is purposeful in our suffering (Romans 8:28–30), and that the doorway of the kingdom is opened with the key of tribulation (Acts 14:22). Trials have a way of driving us to search the statutes of God (Psalm 119:71), which in turn sustain us. The longer the suffering, the more intentionally we should look to and rely on Scripture.

Throughout Carson's battle, God comforted me again and again as I opened His Word. On one especially difficult day, I began reading in the book of Job, only to be struck by the profundity of these words: "He knows the way I take; when He has tried me, I shall come forth as gold" (Job 23:10). Though I could not see God at that moment, this verse reminded me that His eyes were very much on me. In addition, I had new confidence that the Lord was using our family trial for a divine purpose, despite my inability to grasp what it was. The peace of God surrounded me as I dared to believe that Carson and our family would emerge better *after* our ordeal than we were *before*. Through the Bible, God spoke powerfully and consoled deeply when we were hurting the most. He will do the same for you.

The Spirit of Christ

Another means God uses to carry our struggles is greater in subtlety and power. Through the person and work of the Holy Spirit, God exercises His compassion for us while also releasing His comfort in us. Aside from the fact that the presence of God's Spirit is the evidence of genuine salvation (Romans 8:9), hurting believers can live with the awareness that the Spirit of Christ will provide peace and enable endurance through the worst seasons of life. Rightly identified as our Comforter or Helper (John 14:16), the Holy Spirit will help us pray through our pain (Romans 8:26–27), learn from and understand our challenges (1 Corinthians 2:12), bring Scripture to our minds when we need it (John 14:26), comfort and strengthen us with the presence of Christ (Ephesians 3:16–17), and dispense peace and joy despite our circumstances (Romans 14:17). Because of the Spirit we can love those who hurt us, maintain our faithfulness, and persevere with patience despite our anxieties and suffering (Galatians 5:22–23). In addition, the third member of the Trinity reminds us that no earthly trial can damage our eternal inheritance through Jesus Christ (Ephesians 1:13–14).

The Worship of Christ

While it may seem strange to mention worship while considering God's willingness to bear our burdens, Christians should not underestimate the liberating joy and power channeled through the plumb line of praise. When we shift our focus away from our problems to the eternal—to the magnificence of the God we serve—the heaviness that we sometimes carry becomes lighter. Worship enables us to set our minds on things above rather than on those things that are on earth (Colossians 3:2). By focusing on who God *is*, what He *has done*, and all that He *will do*, we find the magnitude of our heartaches diminishing under the weight of His glory.

Psalm 145 extols the goodness of God as an anchor amid the turbulent waves of trouble. King David reminds us, "The LORD is gracious and merciful; slow to anger and great in lovingkindness. The LORD is good to all, and His mercies are over all His works" (145:8–9). Knowing these attributes of God, we can trust Him to sustain us when we fall,

> By focusing on who God *is*, what He *has done*, and all that He *will do*, we find the magnitude of our heartaches diminishing under the weight of His glory.

lift us up when we are low (v. 14), be near us when we call on Him (v. 18), hear our cries as we fear Him (v. 19), and protect those of us who love Him (v. 20). When you cannot understand *why* bad things are happening, you must learn to trust Him *who* is sovereign over your life. Praising God for who He is will remind you that bad things cannot blemish the good Father who loves you.

During a drive from the hospital just a few weeks after we arrived in Memphis, Carson sat in the rear passenger seat, and I could easily see him in the rearview mirror. The two of us were mostly silent, and I was more contemplative than I wanted to be. Unwanted scenarios played in my mind like an old movie reel. Oblivious to my pity party, Carson interrupted my thoughts with a request to turn on the radio. At first, I did not notice the song that was playing. Soon enough, however, the sweet sound of my son's soft voice in the back seat entered my ears as he sang the words of Chris Tomlin's "Our God": "Our God is greater, our God is stronger . . . Our God is Healer, awesome in power."

We finished the song together, and after extolling the sovereignty of our Savior, the problems assailing us did not seem so demoralizing. Praise shifted my focus away from the immediate, allowing me to rest in God's big picture.

In addition, remembering God's faithfulness to us in the past is a powerful weapon of survival in the present. After chronicling the history of Israel during one of their darkest seasons, the prophet Habakkuk recalled the demonstrative power of God throughout the nation's decisive moments and drew this conclusion:

> Though the fig tree should not blossom
> And there be no fruit on the vines,
> Though the yield of the olive should fail

And the fields produce no food,
Though the flock should be cut off from the fold
And there be no cattle in the stalls,
Yet I will exult in the LORD,
I will rejoice in the God of my salvation.

Habakkuk 3:17–18

Translation: The faithfulness of God in the past compels us to honor Him in the present, even when our feelings and circumstances scream otherwise.

No matter what happens today, looking back to God's habitual faithfulness offers us hope during the difficult moments when God's goodness is less obvious. Thus, we are told in the Bible to remember the deeds of the Lord (Psalm 8:3), meditate on His work (Psalm 77:12), and make His actions known (Psalm 105:1). Doing so not only gives us joy and satisfaction over past provisions from the Lord, but also unleashes resolve and endurance for any challenges at hand. Despite their many obstacles when taking possession of the promised land given to them by God, the children of Israel were told to "remember what the LORD your God did to Pharaoh and to all Egypt: the great trials which your eyes saw and the signs and the wonders and the mighty hand and the outstretched arm by which the LORD your God brought you out" (Deuteronomy 7:18–19). Why was this instruction so crucial for dealing with the impediments ahead? Because worshiping God for His past provision enabled them (and us) to walk with God through their present problems.

No wonder we, along with the psalmist, ought to declare, "Bless the LORD, O my soul, and all that is within me, bless His holy name. Bless the LORD, O my soul, and forget none of His benefits" (Psalm 103:1–2). And what are His benefits? He pardons our iniquities (v. 3), heals our diseases (v. 3), shows us lovingkindness and compassion (v. 4), satisfies us with good things (v. 5), and refuses to deal with us in light of our sins (v. 10). Like a runway that propels us higher in devotion and faith, the repeated faithfulness of God in the past demands our attention and worship when life bewilders us. If we won't worship God for what He has already done, we will seldom trust Him despite what He has yet to do.

Finally, we should worship God for all that He promises to do in the future for those who belong to Him. Though we live in a fallen world that is cursed by sin, the Bible promises that God will redeem the entire cosmos before establishing a new heaven and a new earth (Romans 8:21). Because the remade earth will function with the same harmony and purpose that characterized the Garden of Eden, there will be no heartache caused by loved ones or enemies, no sickness born of incurable disease, no stress produced by uncontrollable circumstances. Even better, our greatest enemy will die, as death is abolished (1 Corinthians 15:26) and the grave gives way to the victory of eternal life (1 Corinthians 15:54–55).

As a result, we will live with God forever, and Jesus will wipe away all of our tears and pain (Revelation 21:4). When speaking about these coming realities, Isaiah prophesied of a day when "they will not hurt or destroy in all My holy mountain, for the earth will be full of the knowledge of the LORD as the waters cover the sea" (Isaiah 11:9). No wonder "the sufferings of this present time are not worthy to be compared with the glory that is to be revealed to us" (Romans 8:18). When we worship God for these and other promises yet to be fulfilled, our present struggles wilt under the magnificent shadow of the future. All suffering is temporary when measured against the backdrop of eternity. God's intentions for you are greater than the world's inconveniences around you. So worship God for all that He will do!

DISCUSSION QUESTIONS

1. What are some trite explanations people offer for complex trials, and how can they be offensive?
2. What are examples of dark moments in your life when God was faithful to bear your burdens?
3. How has the body of Christ supported you during seasons of testing?
4. Are there particular Scripture passages that have sustained and comforted you?

FOUR

IT'S NOT ALWAYS ABOUT YOU

His honesty was striking. "I understand why God would do this to *our* family, but why would someone like you face something of this magnitude?" Those were the words of an honest father wrestling to fit his daughter's recent diagnosis with leukemia into his understanding of how and why God allows certain things to happen. His logic was simple: "You are a pastor and should be immune to trials and pain. Those who serve God miraculously enjoy trouble-free living, while those who are less committed struggle with trauma like we're facing."

Theologically, this is the opposite of what the Bible teaches. Yet when life takes a downward turn, our inclination is to measure every incident in a cause-effect relationship. I'd love to tell you that I never felt entitled to a life where cancer did not touch our family, but initially I felt what this burdened father articulated. Looking at my son during those first weeks of chemotherapy elicited a mixture of anger toward God and bewilderment with myself. *Have I done something wrong? Is this the result of my sin? Is my son suffering because of me?*

Questions and emotions like these are likely familiar to you. The nature of personal trials and suffering often leaves us wondering if God is angry with or resentful toward us. Though I do not doubt the level of suffering in your life, or mine for that matter, few have been more qualified to have such thoughts than the Old Testament character Job. The first time we encounter him, Job's life is unraveling at every seam. Then when it appears that his circumstances cannot be any worse, Job's situation spirals again. By learning from his plight, we discover valuable lessons about the nature of the adversities we face.

NOT ALL SUFFERING
IS ABOUT YOU

A cursory reading of Job 2 might feel like a rerun episode of your favorite drama (see Job 1). Closer examination, however, reveals the profound truth that sometimes we suffer for reasons that have nothing to do with us. Though this may seem frustrating, the silver lining is that sometimes more is at stake than our personal comfort and understanding of events that unfold in our lives. Despite his best efforts, Satan could not afflict Job enough to break his faith or commitment to God. After losing all of his livestock, servants, and children, this Old Testament hero remained steadfast in his resolve to trust God. Little did he know, as we seldom do, that another round of tragedy was on the horizon.

When Satan came before God to request permission to harm Job, his sinister intentions became painfully clear. Initially, the charge was that Job's faithfulness was merely the result of God's tangible blessings in his life. Thus, the old serpent chided the Lord with this accusation: "Put forth Your hand now and touch all that he has; he will surely curse You to Your face" (Job 1:11).

Using the same tactic when he approached God a second time, the master accuser highlighted Job's physical health: "Put forth Your hand now, and touch his bone and his flesh; he will curse You to Your face" (2:5).

Initially, these statements appear to demean Job's commitment and integrity. A careful look, however, reveals a much more blasphemous intention. Though Job is the recipient of the collateral damage these accusations create, the real focus of each charge is the glory of God rather than the character of His servant. Intrinsic to each remark is the premise that God must bribe us to secure our allegiance. The devil is mocking the notion that people worship God for who He is by insisting that we only love Him because of what He does for us. The test is more about God's worthiness than Job's faithfulness. What Satan is saying, in essence, is this: "Stop giving Job things and he will curse You to Your face! Remove Your protective hand and he will forsake his commitment! Nothing about You, God, is worthy of worship and glory!" Anxious to prove that God must bribe us for our affection, Satan ridicules the idea that who God is matters more than what God does.

Before his great fall, Satan was heaven's chief angel, responsible for worship. His role was to take the praise of the angels directly to God. This sacred duty was marred, however, by a nefarious hunger for the worship only God received. Seeing himself as more glorious than his Maker, the devil sought greater prominence than God. From this point forward, the father of lies sought to diminish God's glory in order to enhance his own. The assault on Job was nothing more than a futile attempt in a series of narcissistic maneuvers to dethrone the glorious Maker of heaven and earth.

The same agenda later drove the demonic schemes behind the temptations of Jesus. After our Savior had fasted for forty days, Satan tempted Him to turn bread into stones, suggesting that His heavenly Father's provision was unreliable (Matthew 4:3). Next, the wicked one insinuated that the Father's love is undependable. The only way to prove otherwise, he chided, was for Jesus to throw Himself from the top of the temple in order to provoke His divine rescue (4:5–6). Finally, Satan's pretentious goal became vividly apparent when he solicited worship from Jesus in exchange for the kingdoms of the world (4:8–9). Our ancient enemy was, and still is, propagating the lie that God is not really glorious and that Satan is more deserving of worship.

Satan wants to prove that you don't love God simply because of who He is. As strange as it may sound, your trials may have very little to do with you.

Despite our tendency to look insatiably for the cause and effect behind every trial we face, sometimes we are mere background characters in a much bigger story. Even when hardship benefits us personally, the greater battle is one of preserving the glory of God. While it is true that God uses suffering for our good, it is also true that sustained endurance puts God's magnificence on constant display. Yes, we can learn important life lessons during seasons of pain, but even then, the promotion of divine glory is the main agenda. Why is it crucial for us to grasp this principle? One needs to look no further than our typical reactions to difficulty.

God, how could You let this happen to me?
What did I *do to cause this?*
You could have helped me, *Lord, but You didn't!*
I *deserve better than this!*

Certainly, it often feels like the world is against us and that Satan in particular wants to destroy us. The reality, however, is that any demonic attack is not an assault on us personally. The devil wants to ruin your life, not primarily because he hates you, but because he hates God. He wants to prove that you don't love God simply because of who He is. As strange as it may sound, your trials may have very little to do with you.

TRIALS STILL HURT

I know what you might be thinking. *Well, what you're saying may be true for others, but my suffering is so personal and traumatizing that this can't possibly be the case in my situation. If you knew how badly I'm hurting, you would know that what I'm facing is all about me.* Fair enough. But consider carefully what followed for Job. After Satan insisted that any man would curse God after losing his health, God granted His unrelenting foe permission to inflict any level of physical pain short of taking Job's life (Job 2:6).

Because their implications often linger, sickness and physiological problems, perhaps more than anything else, cause us to doubt God. Joni Eareckson Tada contends:

I believe [Satan] views disabilities as his last great stronghold to defame the good character of God. Suffering is that last frontier he exploits to smear God's trustworthiness. The Devil relishes inciting people to complain, "How could a good God allow my child to be born with this horrible defect?" and asking, "How can I trust a God who would permit cancer to take my husband of only six months?"

or wondering, "Why would I believe in a God who includes Alzheimer's and autism in His plans for people?"[1]

Satan's permission to harm Job without killing him also proves where the real battle raged. If maligning God's servant were the goal, the most effective means would have been his death. To the contrary, the only way to embarrass God was for this righteous man to abandon his faith while living. What follows is perhaps the most horrific ordeal any single human being has ever faced, outside of Jesus on the cross. Job had already endured the heartache of losing his children, the anxiety of watching his fortune dwindle, and the unsettling breach of security he previously knew. Now he falls from a picture of health to a pile of bones that would find death a relief. The text simply says, "Then Satan went out from the presence of the LORD and smote Job with sore boils from the sole of his foot to the crown of his head. And he took a potsherd to scrape himself while he was sitting among the ashes" (Job 2:7–8).

We cannot be certain what the primary ailment was. Beyond any doubt, though, is the unsettling image that emerges throughout the story. These boils were pulsating sores from the top of his head to the bottom of his feet. Other symptoms included Job's loss of appetite (3:24), fears and depression (3:25), inability to sleep (7:3), difficulty in breathing (9:18), dark eyelids (16:16), weight loss (19:20), chronic pain (30:27), and high fever (30:30).[2]

---

1. Joni Eareckson Tada, *A Place of Healing: Wrestling with the Mysteries of Suffering, Pain, and God's Sovereignty* (Colorado Springs: Cook, 2010), 30.

2. Noted in Charles Swindoll, *Job: A Man of Heroic Endurance* (Nashville: Word, 2004), 33.

To make matters worse, Job's wife steps onto the scene, only to prompt his blasphemy and certain death (Job 2:9). Tragically, her intended course of action is exactly what the evil one hoped to evoke in Job. The foolishness of her counsel underscores the depth of her personal pain as she watched her husband waste away after also losing her children. From every angle, Job bore the brunt of deep personal pain that few tragedies rival. It doesn't get closer to home than this; yet the subplot had little to do with this man.

Carson was incredibly frail most of the first year.

The same is often true of us. The depth of our pain doesn't guarantee that we are hell's primary target. With Job as a measuring stick, it seems that the deeper our trauma, the higher the eternal stakes. The magnitude of our agony does not necessarily reveal the motive behind our battles. That said, don't confuse the assertion that God's glory is often the main battleground as some stoic denial that every trial takes its toll and causes us deep, sometimes abiding pain. Our suffering isn't always about us, but that doesn't make it hurt any less. Being caught in the crossfire of Satan's unholy war to embarrass God doesn't make our wounds any less piercing. Even though trials aren't necessarily about us, they still work powerfully against us.

During the worst of Carson's battle with leukemia, I always

knew that God could use our pain for good and that He would somehow be glorified as a result of our suffering. I would be less than honest, however, if I did not admit that we still had trouble sleeping at night. I would frequently lie awake, staring at the dark contours of our bedroom, lit only by beams of moonlight shining through our window blinds. Often, out of nowhere, fear paralyzed my heart as I contemplated the worst-case scenario. Some days, feelings of anger, frustration, and panic plagued my mind with such severity that I did not want to get out of bed.

Awareness of a greater purpose behind suffering does not mitigate the realities of walking through it.

I will likely never know the degree to which Carson's trial was for our personal benefit versus the glory of God, but I do know that God's hidden agenda through our heartache did not lessen the burden we felt. You will likely wrestle with the same delicate agony when your life unravels. Awareness of a greater purpose behind suffering does not mitigate the realities of walking through it. Acknowledging our pain, however, will not diminish our appreciation for God's underlying handiwork.

A RADICAL PERSPECTIVE THAT BRINGS HOPE

The above assertions may seem unfair and even cruel. *Why would God allow such adversity? Why does He allow us to be players in Satan's wicked schemes? What if we have no desire to be agents of His glory?* Legitimate questions like these require careful, thoughtful consideration. Thankfully, we have the advantage of listening in as Job responds to his wife.

First, notice that he exposes her (and our) frustrations for what they are—namely, a lack of faith. "You speak as one of the foolish women speaks" (Job 2:10). Literally, he admonishes his wife to stop talking like an unbeliever. Though Job doesn't call her foolish, he does acknowledge that she is speaking like those who are. He then levels a rhetorical question that introduces a radical perspective that we need: "Shall we indeed accept good from God and not accept adversity?" Obviously, the intended answer is no, but think carefully before you respond.

Much like Job's wife, our initial reactions to difficulties are frustration and bewilderment far too frequently. *Where was God when my father died? How could God let me lose my life savings? Why is God allowing my marriage to fall apart?* Questions like these reveal our cynical shortsightedness. We fail to acknowledge God's daily provision in our lives, yet we remain quick to chastise Him when things go wrong. Though we never thank Him for our health, we immediately cry foul when sickness comes upon us. We seldom see time with our family as a precious gift, but we anxiously curse God when the people we love are taken away. The tranquility of beautiful, peaceful days is often lost on us, but any natural disaster causes us to question the goodness of the Lord. Ignoring God when all is well leaves us in a poor position to demand answers from Him when all is not. Questions, though permissible, seem disingenuous when they do not flow out of hearts full of appreciation for all that we do understand about God's work.

In addition, past blessings can empower us to trust God when His actions seem confusing. Have you ever noticed how easily we forget all the times that God protected, delivered, and strengthened us? When God leads us through seasons of difficulty, it is important to remember how faithful He has been in the past. If we forget what God *has done*, we will quickly lament what He *is doing*. We accept adversity from the Lord precisely because our open hands have frequently received His many gifts. Job's perspective reminds us that followers of Christ trust God to bestow blessings we can handle, while also believing He has reasons every time we suffer. Accepting good and bad from the hand of the Lord enables us to endure affliction for a greater good.

Finally, the Bible reveals, "In all this Job did not sin with his lips" (Job 2:10). If you're reading this book, chances are that you or someone you care about is facing a very difficult time. Job's example provides evidence that your life can honor God anyway. Moments of despair can give way to a pattern of hopeful trust. The greater the pain you're facing, the greater the potential for you to glorify God with your life. Ironically, this requires facing your deepest hurts rather than pretending they are not there. God does not expect us to dismiss our anxiety; He wants us to repurpose it instead. By seeking to magnify God's name through our hardships, we demonstrate that every trial, whether about us or not, is part of a greater design that bears eternal significance.

DISCUSSION QUESTIONS

1. Do you sometimes feel more deserving of trials than others?
2. How can the personal nature of calamities cloud your view of God and His agenda?
3. How can God's hidden purposes help you cope with the painful realities you face?

FIVE DON'T WASTE YOUR PAIN

I'll never forget the first time I walked through the front door of the Ronald McDonald House. The seated statue of America's favorite clown did not make me smile. In fact, I felt as if I would never smile again at that point. Despite the cozy warmth of the family room nestled next to the front desk, I lamented my need to be there.

The friendly staff welcomed me with a tour of the facility, but the toys, the paintings, and the posted list of upcoming activities did little to comfort me. A beautiful little girl wearing an oxygen mask and seated in a wheelchair was a painful reminder of what lay ahead. Playing cards at a table was a family gathered around their son, whose bald head glowed from the sun coming through the window. I noticed the swollen cheeks of another little boy, no older than four, who zipped by me in the hallway. Sitting with her face to the wall was a teenage girl who was obviously trying to hide her left side, most of which was missing due to the invasive surgeries she had undergone.

I listened to rules, signed an agreement, and was handed a set of keys. This would be our new home for the next five weeks. I loved the mission of the Ronald McDonald House, but I could not believe it was necessary for my family to be there. Carson's diagnosis was only seven days old at that point, and I was still reeling from the shock and dismay of our lives being violently interrupted.

Those first seven days in the hospital are a bit of a blur to me. Carson began chemotherapy almost immediately, and it continued nearly every day. Next, we learned that the duration of his treatment would extend for about two and a half years (134 weeks). Through three phases of protocol, varying degrees of intensity and numerous drugs awaited him. Though the majority of his chemotherapy came just once per week, the first six weeks required daily care and multiple doses every other day. Designed to shock the body into remission, this induction phase of treatment is crucial for the treatment of acute lymphoblastic leukemia. Contrary to our initial expectation, however, this did not mean a six-week hospital stay. After seven days of inpatient care, Carson moved from the safety of his hospital room to the Ronald McDonald House just across the street.

Initially, this change unleashed a new cycle of anxiety in my heart. Our room was nice enough, but I feared germs, Carson's restricted diet, potential fevers, and living among strangers. With a sink, a bathroom, two beds, and a reading chair, this felt like a hotel to me, and I couldn't imagine living in this environment with a son who had cancer. Though Heather and Carson were waiting for me at the hospital, anxious for a change of scenery, I sat down in the brown leather chair by the window and began to cry uncontrollably. This was the first time I had been alone since arriving in Memphis, and I simply could not hold it back. My composure was gone, and the emotions I felt were demoralizing. *How can we survive this? What about all of our responsibilities at home? After these first six weeks, how can we travel to Memphis for another 128 consecutive weeks of additional chemotherapy? Even more important, can we win this battle? Is Carson going to live, or will he die?*

TOO PAINFUL TO WASTE

Shortly after moving into our temporary home, I phoned a mentor and friend in Kentucky who continues to play a pivotal role in my relationship with Christ and in my ministry. As I described the despair I felt, he responded deliberately by saying, "Remember, some things are just too painful to waste." Like the jagged edge of a shoreline for a vagabond adrift at sea, those words were piercing and comforting at the same time. Immediately, I realized the road ahead might grow worse before improving, but I was suddenly determined to leverage the horror of our new reality for a greater good. My new goal was to yield to God's plan in order to become the best Christian I could be.

Having already seen that many of the challenges we shoulder are often less about us specifically and more about the integrity and glory of God generally, we might initially consider growing through trials to be a competing thought. Despite the divine backdrop that accompanies the certain calamities of a fallen world, however, we should not conclude that trials cannot change us for the better. Even when God's *primary* agenda is the beauty of His name, oftentimes a *secondary* result is the development of His saints. There is no dichotomy, in my view, between the development of Christian character through adversity and the magnifying of God's glory through the same. Thus, even if God were seeking to glorify Himself through our family,

I determined to learn all I could and grow as much as possible through the ordeal ahead.

Much more than wishful thinking, this approach to enduring adversity is remarkably consistent with the message of Scripture. Romans 8:28 assures, "And we know that God causes all things to work together for good to those who love God, to those who are called according to His purpose." In every circumstance, in every struggle, in every heartache life throws our way, God actively works for the good of those who belong to Him. Bad developments, tragic occurrences, depressing realities, shocking events, and even evil actions have a sense of intentionality because of God's redemptive agenda for His children. *Nothing* comes across the pages of our lives that God doesn't utilize for a greater purpose. And what is that purpose? God causes all things *to work together for good*. In other words, He meticulously puts the pieces of our existence together to produce something of benefit to us. But how do trials work for our benefit? What good could possibly come out of the unease our sorrows cause?

SILVER LININGS IN DARK PLACES

Surveying the various good outcomes God frequently produces from our agonies requires a careful word of caution. Because knowing the mind of God is impossible (Romans 11:33–34), discerning His intentions demands humility. Though it is true that God may have a singular goal for our afflictions, His desired end is often multifaceted and complex. You may understand something of God's design for your hardships, but the full breadth of His intentions is often incomprehensible. Grasping for understanding of what God might be teaching you is commendable, but speaking dogmatically for Him is not. We should be proactive in order to grow, without being presumptuous regarding the Lord. With these boundaries in place, the following list is by no means comprehensive. These are just *some* of the beneficial results God brings into our lives through our suffering.

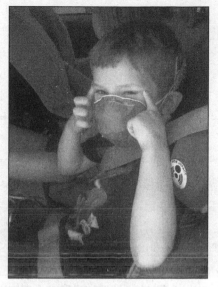

"Hey, Dad, I'm smiling with my eyes!"

Trials Grow and Strengthen Our Faith

Because God is more concerned with our character than our comfort, sometimes He chooses to use calamity in order to sanctify us. James 1:2–4 explains: "Consider it all joy, my brethren, when you encounter various trials, knowing that the testing of your faith produces endurance. And let endurance have its perfect result, so that you may be perfect and complete, lacking in nothing."

If ease or happiness is your primary goal in life, you will likely feel frustrated and betrayed when God chooses to deepen your maturity through a trial. The potential for meaningful development and growth, however, may be greatest when we are hurting the most. Will you eagerly follow a God who will likely break you in order to mature your commitment to Him?

73

Before Carson was sick, I confess that my life was relatively easy—no major heartache and few serious problems to weather. This first real challenge to my faith tested everything I said I believed. Even though I had preached for more than a decade with an adequate knowledge of the Scriptures, suddenly my situation forced me to reckon with my confidence in the fundamentals of my faith. Surface faith will not suffice when circumstances threaten what you treasure most in life. I am thankful that throughout our dilemma, my confidence in God's truth only deepened. Before I might have told you what I believe about Christianity. Today I can tell you what I know from firsthand experience.

Trials Deepen Our Fellowship with Jesus and Reveal His Strength

When speaking about his primary goal for living, the apostle Paul reminds disciples of Jesus of the need to seek to "know Him and the power of His resurrection and the fellowship of His sufferings, being conformed to His death" (Philippians 3:10). Though most of us are eager to experience the power of Christ's resurrection, we are less enthusiastic about the fellowship of His sufferings. Do not forget, however, that the agony of Golgotha preceded the glory of His victory over the grave. As we learned previously, experiencing the power of Christ's resurrection begins on the road of heartache (see chapter 2).

In a similar way, receiving God's power in our lives will require enduring great wounds without wavering. Apart from suffering, we simply cannot learn about God or relate to Him on an intimate level. Believing that God is real and present is one thing; trusting that He is enough, no matter what we face, is another thing entirely.

Though we are quite capable of cognitively grasping these ideas, we cannot embrace them fully until we experience their reality for ourselves. Trials force us to move beyond superficial knowledge of Jesus into a meaningful, daily walk with Him.

Even those who believe the gospel and claim a relationship with God sometimes fail to live in light of their commitment. Tragically, though we know God is there, we seldom feel like we need Him. Before Carson's diagnosis, I often preached about the peace of God, but I seldom felt like I needed it. My prayer life was consistent, but it left much to be desired. I read my Bible to prepare sermons, but I rarely did so with desperation to hear from the Lord. My outward obedience was, at times, lacking the inward fellowship with God that I now crave.

> **Trials force us to move beyond superficial knowledge of Jesus into a meaningful, daily walk with Him.**

Maybe you can relate. Do you pray more when times are tough? Is your Bible always close by when you are searching for answers? Is your church worship attendance noticeably more frequent when things have gone awry in your life? Why are these patterns so apparent? Stated simply, it's because suffering forces us to live what we really believe. Thus, the Lord beckons us into a deeper, more meaningful fellowship with Jesus through the doorway of hardship. In our weakness, we move from having a cognitive awareness of His strength to experiencing the personal peace it brings.

Trials Increase Our Effectiveness in Serving Others

We seldom consider how our current struggles might prepare us for future service, yet God often equips us to serve others as a result of our most painful experiences. In 2 Corinthians 1:4, we learn that

God the Father "comforts us in all our affliction so that we will be able to comfort those who are in any affliction with the comfort with which we ourselves are comforted by God." In addition to the personal benefit God produces, the fruit of adversity in our lives will often bear the seeds of comfort for other hurting believers along the way. The Lord's intention to comfort us is also His investment in bearing the pain of others who are not even hurting yet. When we enjoy the supernatural peace that surpasses our understanding today, we become distributors of that same consolation to others tomorrow and every day thereafter (Philippians 4:7).

Today I regularly receive calls from other pastors and churches whenever a child they know is diagnosed with cancer of some sort. Though I was completely unaware of it at the time, God was giving my wife and me the gift of His comfort so that we could share it with other hurting people. Your trials will enable you to do the same.

Trials Are Often a Powerful Means to Spread the Gospel

It may seem counterintuitive, but our most powerful opportunities to be witnesses for Jesus will often come when our lives are falling apart. Because unbelievers frequently dismiss Christianity as unnecessary at best or a crutch at worst, observing faithful saints who suffer well is a powerful jolt of reality that opens wayward hearts to the claims of Christ. Despite being in prison for preaching the gospel, the apostle Paul assured the Philippians, "My circumstances have turned out for the greater progress of the gospel, so that my imprisonment in the cause of Christ has become well known throughout the whole praetorian guard and to everyone else" (Philippians 1:12–13).

Day after day, week after week, month after month, this missionary warhorse faithfully shared the good news of salvation with every person who entered his prison. As guards changed shifts every six to eight hours, God's servant enthusiastically declared the joyful message of God's loving sacrifice for sins on the cross to at least three or four individuals each day. Imagine their surprise after these guards expected to be met by a defeated prisoner, only to encounter a joyful man still serious about his faith in and walk with his Savior. Can you imagine the far-reaching impact of Paul's steadfast commitment?

It may seem counterintuitive, but our most powerful opportunities to be witnesses for Jesus will often come when our lives are falling apart.

In a similar way, God breathes power into our afflictions when we use them as a doorway to the gospel. Because there were so many hurting families at the Ronald McDonald House who could not leave the property to attend weekly church services, we decided to hold a Sunday morning service in the chapel while we stayed there. Each week, I prayed that God would speak through me to convey the strong foundation that was unshaken despite our son's diagnosis. *How do you remain so strong? What do you have that I don't?* and *Maybe there is something to this God thing* were common responses we heard.

When non-Christians encounter the sustaining faith of a weary saint, it is powerfully inspirational. Three people, whom I never would have met apart from our worst earthly circumstance, came to Christ over a period of five weeks simply because trials opened doors for us to share the gospel. Though few will ever admit it, many friends and acquaintances will be watching closely to see if Christ makes any difference in your life when you are hurting the most. Perhaps we suffer at times just for them.

Trials Embolden Other Christians to Be Courageous for Christ

Similar to its impact on those outside of Christianity, resolute commitment to the Lord despite adverse realities is a powerful motivator for other believers as well. Again, God's servant to the Gentiles is a powerful example of maximizing our deepest moments of despair for the kingdom of God. Philippians 1:14 celebrates this: "Most of the brethren, trusting in the Lord because of my imprisonment, have far more courage to speak the word of God without fear." In other words, Paul's devotion to Christ in prison was a powerful influence on believers who were not suffering. Those who were less committed were challenged to devote their lives to the gospel because one man was willing to serve God under any circumstance.

Think about the Christians who inspire you the most. Chances are you watched them walk through a season of difficulty without wavering. When I was a boy, my favorite teacher fought a brain tumor for nearly four years. This giant of a man demonstrated the substance of Christianity to me in a profound way. Before one of his surgeries, he sat me down in the hallway of my elementary school one day and declared, "I am not afraid to die, and you won't be either if you will live every day of your life for Jesus Christ." That conversation still impacts me today. Mr. A, as we called him, ultimately lost his earthly battle with cancer, but he is still enjoying his heavenly reward for such profound faithfulness. His life emboldened me to give myself more fully to my Savior. Your suffering may allow you to do the same for someone else.

Trials Can Be a Form of Discipline
Intended to Produce Repentance

No Christian will ever experience the condemnation of God (Romans 8:1). However, Scripture explicitly teaches that God does discipline those who belong to Him. Hebrews 12:9–11 reminds us:

> Furthermore, we had earthly fathers to discipline us, and we respected them; shall we not much rather be subject to the Father of spirits, and live? For they disciplined us for a short time as seemed best to them, but He disciplines us for our good, so that we may share His holiness. All discipline for the moment seems not to be joyful, but sorrowful; yet to those who have been trained by it, afterwards it yields the peaceful fruit of righteousness.

Sometimes trials are the consequences of our sinful choices and actions. Other times our adversities may not be directly traceable to a specific moment of disobedience, but God intends to produce greater holiness within us nonetheless. God loves us too much to ignore any behavior or perspective that would push us away from Him. Like a loving father, He carefully and expeditiously works to correct us when we stray. Though this involvement in our lives can be painful at times, it proves God's *affection for* us rather than His *abandonment of* us.

WHY DOES IT STILL HURT?

Again, these are merely *some* of the ways God uses our suffering, not a comprehensive list of *all* the ways. Still, we now have a better sense of how God works our hardships for good. Before moving on, let me offer a necessary word of caution. Acknowledging God's purposes behind what we face should not be viewed as a passive denial of the severity surrounding our circumstances. While it is true that God promises to use everything we face to accomplish good (Romans 8:28), this does not mean that everything we go through is good. The ultimate goal and benefit certainly are, but the pathway toward God's good outcome is often quite painful.

And what is God's ultimate ambition for each of us as difficulties move in and out of our lives unexpectedly? What is the common denominator of every purpose behind our hardships? Simply put, it's to make you more like His Son, Jesus. After the assuring promise of God's good intentions for His people, the Bible assures, "For those whom He foreknew, He also predestined to become conformed to the image of His Son" (Romans 8:29). Every trial we face has the potential to make us more like Jesus Christ. Even when God does not change your circumstances, you can be certain that He will actively change your character. Only eternity will reveal the manifold goodness wrought out of our greatest tragedies.

Even when God does not change your circumstances, you can be certain that He will actively change your character.

I know it's easy to disagree. Sometimes the weight of our anxiety causes our faith to buckle under the pressure of doubt. Perhaps you cannot see any possible good coming out of the burdens you are carrying. Maybe you're thinking . . .

- **But I've been mistreated.** Read Genesis 50:20: "You meant evil against me, but God meant it for good in order to bring about this present result."

- **But I've suffered more than most.** Drink deep from Romans 8:18: "I consider that the sufferings of this present time are not worthy to be compared with the glory that is to be revealed to us."
- **But I'm lonely and afraid.** Remember Romans 8:39: "[Nothing] will be able to separate us from the love of God, which is in Christ Jesus our Lord."
- **But I'm close to death.** Lean hard on Philippians 1:21: "For to me, to live is Christ and to die is gain."

God is working. Believe and trust Him. Even if good days are not ahead, He will complete His good work in you.

DISCUSSION QUESTIONS

1. Have you, like the author, ever faced a trial so severe that its accompanying emotions resurfaced repeatedly?
2. How do the potential outcomes of your burdens encourage you?
3. What other positive consequences might emerge after the dust of your anxieties settles?
4. How can you maintain your eternal hope when your earthly challenges discourage you?

SIX | HANGING ON FOR DEAR LIFE

A gentle breeze pushed us along the sidewalk under the canopy of what was shaping up to be a beautiful sunny day in Memphis. On the surface, this morning was no different from the forty-one others that preceded it. For the previous six weeks, living in the Ronald McDonald House across the street from St. Jude became our routine. Most days we would wake up early, have breakfast, and then make our way to the hospital for blood work or chemotherapy.

Treating childhood leukemia requires three phases of treatment with varying degrees of aggressiveness. The first, commonly called *induction*, seeks to shock the body into remission with aggressive cocktails of complementary drugs. For six straight weeks, Carson received eight different medications for a total of thirty-five treatments across the span of forty-two days. This same time period also included twenty-eight consecutive days of receiving the steroid prednisone. On day fifteen, a bone marrow draw revealed that the strategy was working, but leukemia cells were still in his body. Though the progress was good, it also meant a second test was necessary before we could say Carson was in remission. Today was that day.

A PROMISE THAT CHANGES EVERYTHING

Although many anxieties plagued our family during this time, the most terrifying did not call into question *what* God could do, but *where* God was. After the shock of the initial diagnosis wore off, the mundane rhythm of watching our son live with cancer was debilitating. His thick, shiny hair fell out. His face was continually swollen from the prednisone that was boosting his immune system. His moods were fragile, even volatile at times. His disposition not only was contrary to what we had grown to expect, but also left us wondering if we would ever have our normal son again.

We prayed for Carson's healing, but heaven seemed deafeningly silent. Promises from Scripture were less vivid, and it began to feel like we were on our own. The routine of Carson's treatment gave us focus, but it also bore the mirage of finality. We felt trapped and alone with no end in sight. Whereas God's fingerprints adorned nearly every part of our lives just weeks prior, now it seemed as if the Lord had saturated our dilemma with His absence.

Carson's second bone marrow draw went exactly as planned, but waiting on the test results to see if he was in remission was the worst. It only took two days for the report to come back, but those forty-eight hours seemed eternal. What if the chemotherapy did not work? How could my son survive if his body was not responding to his treatment? Our fears were palpable. If these test results showed anything other than the complete absence of cancer, drastic measures would be necessary. Though I aggressively prayed for good news from our doctor, my heart was void of peace, and fear dominated my mind. *What if the cancer is still there? What other options do we have left? Can Carson's little body handle much more?* Thoughts like these flooded my soul with dread and timidity. Next I began to question the Lord. *Where is God in all of this? Why does He seem so distant when we need Him the most?*

Then I read it. The verse was not new to me, but I had never been in a situation where I needed it quite like this moment. "The LORD is the one who goes ahead of you; He will be with you. He will not fail you or forsake you. Do not fear or be dismayed" (Deuteronomy 31:8). These ancient words of assurance were first passed from Moses to Joshua during the pivotal transition from one leader to another as Israel followed God to their promised land. Yet their certitude and solace still undergird weary believers today in need of an unshakable promise due to the storms of life. And what is that promise? *God is always with us, even when we do not realize it.* Not only does God go *before us* when challenges are on the horizon, but He also remains *with us* as we walk through our most agonizing troubles. But how can we be so sure? Joshua certainly enjoyed the security of the Lord's presence, but why should we have confidence that these words remain applicable to Christ-followers today?

A PROMISE THAT IS TIMELESS IN ITS SCOPE

Thankfully, God's pledge to Joshua was not an isolated incident. Moses' successor reminded God's people of the same promise as they fought against their enemies (Joshua 10:25). Before King

Solomon built Israel's temple in Jerusalem, his father David assured him that God would never fail or forsake him until the work was finished (1 Chronicles 28:20). After Assyria invaded Judah with intentions of conquering Jerusalem, King Hezekiah admonished his citizens by insisting that the Lord was with them and that He is greater than any enemy they faced (2 Chronicles 32:7–8).

Every time a leader relayed the promise of God's presence to others, a clear call to be strong and courageous followed. Not only was this the pattern employed by Moses as he encouraged Joshua, God Himself follows the same progression three times as He speaks directly to His new leader (see Joshua 1).

- *Be strong and courageous* . . . for I will give the people the land I promised (v. 6).
- *Be strong and courageous* . . . as you obey My commandments (v. 7).
- *Be strong and courageous* . . . because I will be with you wherever you go (v. 9).

These appeals to strength and courage are the direct result of God's repeated intention to remain with Joshua no matter the situation. The Lord assured him, "No man will be able to stand before you all the days of your life. Just as I have been with Moses, I will be with you; I will not fail you or forsake you" (Joshua 1:5).

God frequently reassured His children by directly asserting His presence with them. When temptation assailed Abraham, the Lord promised to be a shield for him (Genesis 15:1). As Isaac endured the envy and hostility of others, God again guaranteed His presence (Genesis 26:24). While the Jewish people served under harsh circumstances due to the Babylonian threat, God maintained His intention to save and deliver them (Jeremiah 42:11). Though the apostle Paul suffered greatly for serving His Savior, the Lord again acknowledged His presence and admonished the apostle not to fear (Acts 18:9–10). Even while the people of Judah faced the self-inflicted consequences of their rebellion, God came to them with compassion, saying, "Do not fear, for I am with you" (Isaiah 41:10; 43:5).

In addition to these stated examples of Yahweh's determination to remain with His people at all times, the Bible often observes that God is with His servants even when He does not say so. Consider again the escalating hardships of Joseph (see chapter 1). The Genesis narrative reveals that his brothers hated him. After they sold him into slavery, Potiphar's wicked wife falsely accused Joseph of adulterous intentions, resulting in an unfair prison sentence. Yet, despite God's apparent silence on the matter, the Bible continually assures us of God's involvement (emphases mine):

- "*The LORD was with Joseph*, so he became a successful man" (Genesis 39:2).
- "His master saw that *the LORD was with him*" (39:3).
- "*The LORD was with Joseph* and extended kindness to him, and gave him favor in the sight of the chief jailer" (39:21).
- "The chief jailer did not supervise anything under Joseph's charge *because the LORD was with him*; and whatever he did, *the LORD made to prosper*" (39:23).

Joseph seemed to lean hard into the reality of God's presence. Toward the end of his life, while looking back over his most painful events, he finds comfort in knowing that what others meant for evil against him, God strategically used for good (see Genesis 50:20).

If these examples still seem too far from the world in which you live, drink deeply from the profound insight of Acts 17:27–28, which assures us that God is "not far from each one of us" because "in Him we live and move and exist." Our heavenly Father invites us to enjoy contentment apart from financial or material ambitions simply because He promises to never desert or forsake us (Hebrews 13:5), to always be our helper in every situation (13:6). In addition, Jesus, when speaking directly to all Christians in every age, guarantees His presence in our lives as we go about the work of making disciples of the nations (Matthew 28:18–20). Regardless of how severe our misfortunes might be, we can rest easy, knowing that God "does not forsake His godly ones" (Psalm 37:28). He is *always* with us!

THE VALUE OF A GOOD MEMORY

Once we understand that God is active and present in our lives at all times, we can find comfort in His presence when everything around us begins to fall apart. But how is that possible? How can we move beyond merely believing that God has not forsaken us to actually finding refuge in His presence as a result? A good memory is the key to finding rest when the fallenness of creation interrupts, and even robs us of, the peaceful existence we crave. Perhaps returning to our first example will prove helpful.

The assurance of God's abiding presence in our lives actually

appeared long before Moses faded off the scene in order for Joshua
to emerge as Israel's new leader. The reason the Bible repeats
this promise in Deuteronomy 31
is because God's people refused to
live in light of its truth forty years
before this historic setting. The
Old Testament book of Numbers
records one of the greatest blun-
ders God's people ever committed.

A good memory is the key to finding rest when the fallenness of creation robs us of the peaceful existence we crave.

When Moses sent twelve spies into the promised land that the
Lord wanted to give them as a home, all but two came back saying the people in the region were too big and strong for them to
seize the territory. Only Joshua and Caleb resisted the majority
by pleading, "If the LORD is pleased with us, then He will bring
us into this land and give it to us—a land which flows with milk
and honey. Only do not rebel against the LORD; and do not fear
the people of the land, for they will be our prey. Their protection
has been removed from them, and the LORD is with us; do not
fear them" (Numbers 14:8–9).

Note the confident insistence that there was nothing to fear
because God was with His people. Why were these two servants
so certain? How did Joshua and Caleb know that God would not
forsake them despite the great odds they faced? Better still, how
can we be just as sure? When doubt assaults our confidence about
what God *will do* in the present and future, faith compels us to
look back and remember what God has *already done* in the past.

Cowering under the pressure of what we need from God
will leave us forgetful of what He has already provided for us.
Thus, God wants us to remember His previous faithfulness while
we are trying to make sense of today. In fact, listen to God's

indignation over Israel's long-term memory loss: "The LORD said to Moses, 'How long will this people spurn Me? And how long will they not believe in Me, despite all the signs which I have performed in their midst?'" (Numbers 14:11).

What were the miracles God was referring to? Why was there no room for His people to doubt that He was with them? Consider the signs of God's presence leading up to the acquisition of the promised land:

- God sent ten plagues upon Egypt (blood, frogs, gnats, flies, dead livestock, boils, hail, locusts, darkness, and the death of the firstborn son) so that Pharaoh would let the Israelites go.
- He parted the Red Sea for them to walk across on dry land.
- He gave them water to drink from a rock at Meribah.
- He gave them manna from heaven to eat.
- He led them with a cloud during the day and a pillar of fire at night.
- He defeated their enemies at Amalek and Rephidim as long as Moses' arms were held up.
- He gave the Ten Commandments as Mount Sinai shook, covering it with smoke and surrounding it with thunder and lightning.

Yet, despite miracle after miracle, these stubborn people refused to believe God and doubted His presence among them. Before we cast a judgmental eye toward our spiritual ancestors, however, we need to acknowledge our tendency to do the same. Despite the repeated faithfulness of God, all too often we quickly forget. If we doubt that God is with us, it may well be because we have forgotten all that God has already done for us. He wants us to remember, but we seldom do when life unravels.

Is it any wonder that forty years later, Moses would remind them of the same promise they had rejected so many years ago? Again, God's chosen people were on the verge of claiming His promise, but this time it was Joshua, not the steady leader the people already knew and trusted, who would take them into the land. Seasons of transition can create a sense of panic and abiding fear as we consider the possibilities of what might be ahead. Perhaps you can relate? Is a new job or an unfamiliar surrounding keeping you up at night? Has a new season of life forced you to face role reversals or the loss of a meaningful relationship? Do signs of declining health leave you wondering why God is nowhere to be found? The rhythmic evolution of our circumstances begs for an affirmation or guarantee that God will not forsake us when we need Him most.

Thankfully, God's past faithfulness shouts over the invasive agonies we face. Note Moses' reassurances as he positions the people for what is ahead. Deuteronomy 31:3 emphasizes, "It is the LORD your God who will cross ahead of you." Not only is God present *where you are*; He is also busy at work in the place *where you are going*. In fact, He is ahead of every problem, every challenge, and every dark cloud that looms on our horizon. In this moment and every moment ahead, God will never forsake His people.

As Carson's treatment progressed, even the details of our trial gave continual reassurance of God's abiding steadfastness in our lives. Because our pediatrician was familiar with St. Jude after serving a previous patient, our transition to the world's leading

Dr. Pui became Carson's friend and hero.

research hospital for pediatric cancer was seamless. Once there, our primary physician was a man widely recognized as the leading oncologist in the treatment of childhood leukemia, Dr. Ching-Hon Pui. I have no doubt that God orchestrated these events for the good of my son. In addition, the Lord surrounded us with the right people to bring us real comfort. On my staff was a father whose daughter had been a patient at St. Jude more than thirty years previously. His insightful encouragement was a lifeline during our worst moments. Such details illustrate that God protected Carson before and after his diagnosis. Despite the uncertainty of the final outcome, there was no reason to doubt God's involvement in our lives.

Need more evidence of God's presence? Consider the airtight logic Moses passed on as the Israelites faced their fears: "The LORD will do to them just as He did to Sihon and Og, the kings of the Amorites, and to their land, when He destroyed them. The LORD will deliver them up before you, and you shall do to them according to all the commandments which I have commanded you" (Deuteronomy 31:4–5).

Did you catch it? God's previous actions and previous promises were the comforting evidence. Just as the Lord defended His people against their enemies before, He was willing and eager to do so again. The same is true today. If you feel alone or discouraged because of what you see with your eyes, open the windows of your memory and look deep inside for the relentless faithfulness of God. If He did not forsake you *before*, He will not do so *today*.

I imagine it may not be so simple for you. Perhaps the severity of your plight has led you to conclude:

I know I'm going under this time!

I cannot deal with it anymore!

I cannot handle this sickness!

I cannot handle this stress!

I cannot make ends meet!

Too much has changed. It's different this time!

Or maybe you are asking:

God, did You hear what she said?

God, did You see what he did?

God, do You know how I feel?

God, where are You?

You may even wonder if God has really done that much for you. *If I had witnessed the breadth of miracles the Israelites saw in the wilderness,* you reason, *I would not doubt the Lord like I do.*

Visceral feelings like these are understandable, but they are deceptive nonetheless. When problems surface, our minds tend to play tricks on us. Our memories of God's faithfulness fade as doubts and questions about the present replace them. The Israelites doubted God's commitment to them, despite the signs and miracles they observed previously. Their lack of belief was not due to a shortage of evidence that God is always faithful.

Likewise, the trauma of our experiences can sometimes diminish the accuracy and power of our spiritual recollection.

When we bemoan our present realities, it is difficult to appreciate our past victories. Despite ample proof that God *was* and *is* with us throughout our lives, we dangerously call the Lord's character into question when we refuse to remember all that He has done for us. Though God wants us to recall His previous intervention in our lives, we often ridicule His present intentions for us when we are hurting.

Do you find it hard to believe that the Lord is willing to walk with you through every trial? Even if heartache racks your life beyond what seems reasonable, take a moment to remember the numerous demonstrations of God's love for you and His pursuit of you. Remember the sacrificial determination that heaven displayed in order to save you:

- how God the Father raised up a nation called Israel for the sole purpose of producing a Messiah.
- how God sent His only begotten Son into the world by way of a virgin's womb.
- how Jesus was born in the right place at the right time to the right person.
- how God the Son traded the wealth of heaven for the poverty of Bethlehem.
- how our Savior lived a perfect life, though He was in all ways tempted as we are.
- how Jesus was silent while His own people rejected Him.
- how as a lamb being led to the slaughter Jesus stood still while the Romans beat Him.
- how Jesus endured the cross while despising its shame.
- how blood dripped from Jesus' wounds as hell's nails pierced His hands and feet.

- how God the Father bruised His own Son in order to receive you as His own.
- how Jesus bled and died and rose again.
- how Jesus left in order to prepare a place for you so that where He is you may be also.
- how God the Father sent the Holy Spirit to comfort, guide, and teach you all things.
- how Jesus promised that one day He will come again in order to receive you.

While there are definitely seasons when it is challenging to feel God's love, choose to remember what God has already done for you. As you think about the eternal motive and purpose behind your present dilemma, trust the established historical verdict that proves God has no intention of leaving you now. When the doctor says cancer. When your spouse says divorce. When your boss says today is your last day. When your friend says so long. *Do not be afraid. God is with you!*

He was certainly there for us. Just two days after being reminded of the Lord's resolute faithfulness, the call finally came. It was my wife, Heather's, twenty-eighth birthday, and she only wanted one thing. Just six weeks after arriving at St. Jude for the first time, the test showed that the minimal residual disease (MRD) left in Carson's bone marrow was 0 percent—just as we had prayed, he was now in remission! Though God felt strangely absent in the weeks before this news, He remained meticulously active in our lives nonetheless. Even greater than *what* He did, however, was *where* He was. God never left our side. Those test results only highlighted what was true, regardless of the news we received. He was always with us; and He promises to be with you as well.

DISCUSSION QUESTIONS

1. At what point in your life has God felt the most absent to you?

2. How does the assurance of God's sustained presence relieve the fears surrounding your troubles?

3. When has remembering what God did for you in the past helped you trust who God is in the present?

4. How do your feelings betray you when you are under great strain?

5. Does the work of Jesus on the cross prove God's presence with you today?

SEVEN

LIFE WITH AN UNINVITED GUEST

When I finally found my seat on the plane, I could not hold back the tears. My breath was still heavy, and beads of sweat covered my forehead from running through the airport terminal with a suitcase in one hand and my son in the opposite arm. Carson's bald head glistened under the glow of the overhead lights, the reflection broken only by the cartoon Spider-Man strap that held his medical mask in place. Tears were still on his cheeks and his arms still held me tight. He grimaced in pain as I tried to pry him away in order to strap him into the seat beside me. I felt the internal stares of other passengers, though none dared to allow their gaze to land on us. By this time, however, I did not care.

How can we keep this pace? When will Carson feel better? How much more can he take? When is this trial going to end? Thoughts like these imprisoned my mind as I wept uncontrollably. Months had passed since we celebrated Carson's remission, and now it seemed like we were floundering again.

Though this scenario was not typical, it was predictable each month due to a particular medication Carson received. Vincristine helped keep the cancer away, but it also caused

Carson's joints to ache, and the more he moved, the worse the pain became. Mingled with this intrusive chemical was a new (to us) steroid called dexamethasone, designed to relieve the inflammation. Unfortunately, however, it also completely altered our son's disposition, leaving him moody, short-tempered, and even aggressively angry at times.

Today was no different. After coming up the escalator at the Atlanta airport, we began walking toward our flight gate, which was at the very end of the terminal. Carson was already tired, but when his legs began to hurt, he lost all control. Soon he was shouting in frustration, crying to go home, and refusing to move another inch. With our gate so far away and our plane already boarding, I feared we might miss our connection. As I picked him up and began sprinting down the terminal, he cried louder and his body went limp. The discouragement in my heart was the only sensation that rivaled the pain in my arms and legs. It seemed to me that we were a sinking ship, with no rescue in sight.

How can our situation seem so unbearable after so much progress? The news of Carson's remission from leukemia catapulted us to an emotional high that lasted for weeks. With the cancer cells out of his body, whatever was ahead seemed like a mere footnote for a greater battle that had already been won. Reality soon set in, however, as the taxing grind of Carson's treatment plan began to take its toll on us. Few people realize that pediatric leukemia has an extremely high probability of returning. To avoid a relapse, more than two years of additional care is necessary even after the cancer cells are no longer in the body.

Though the second phase, *consolidation*, was only eight weeks in duration, the medications were stronger and had more potentially adverse side effects. Each dosage required a multiday hospital stay to ensure Carson's safety in the event of a severe reaction. Waiting through those moments was traumatic, but with the completion of each successful chemotherapy visit, our confidence grew. Already, though, we were physically and emotionally exhausted. Nothing could have prepared us for the twenty-eight-month marathon that was coming.

The final phase of Carson's protocol, often referred to as *continuation*, was 120 consecutive weeks of grueling trips to the

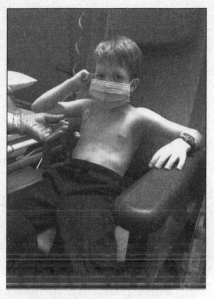

Becoming a pro at accessing his port

hospital in Memphis from our Alabama home every Tuesday and Wednesday. Each week, we flew out of Pensacola, Florida, had a brief layover in Atlanta, and then boarded a plane for Memphis. After we arrived, Carson had blood work on Tuesday evenings to prepare for chemotherapy the following day. We'd get up early the next morning, visit with his doctor, endure his therapy, grab a quick bite to eat, and then board a shuttle back to the airport so we could reverse the itinerary in order to be home by Wednesday evening.

Every week, like clockwork, this routine dictated every part of our lives. A paper road map outlined each week of *continuation*, but with more than two years of treatment remaining, it felt like a never-ending burden. Though we checked off each visit in order to show how far we had come, it seemed like our nightmare would never end.

WHEN THERE IS NO END IN SIGHT

One of the more difficult challenges when weathering trials is the blinding perception that our struggles will plague us forever. Much of the emotional baggage born in adversity is tied to the false notion that our trials are here to stay. The heat of affliction has a way of melting our dreams and consuming the joys of living. With no end in sight, we often face the uncharted waters of depression as waves of anxiety beat against our fragile hearts. Let me share a few reminders to help you cope when there is no light at the end of your tunnel.

Most Trials Are Temporary

Though it seldom feels like it at the time, most of the adversities we face are only temporary. The majority of our problems are not permanent experiences. Have you heard the popular expression "this too shall pass"? Well, it's popular for a reason—it usually does pass. Chances are, you *will* come out on the other side of whatever you are facing. This simple reminder was a constant motivation for me during the uncertain days of Carson's battle. As King David eloquently stated so long ago, "I would have despaired unless I had believed that I would see the goodness of the LORD in the land of the living" (Psalm 27:13). Knowing the temporary nature of our dilemmas frees us to look for the goodness of God beyond the current havoc we face.

Yes, in rare instances, earthly troubles endure for a lifetime. And conflict resolution does not guarantee an end to ongoing difficulties. Even God's most powerful apostle possessed a thorn in his flesh throughout the span of his ministry. Despite Paul's pleas to the contrary, his affliction did not go away (2 Corinthians 12:7–9). In a fallen world, not only do pain and heartache exist, but they manifest in what can appear to be unfair quantities for certain people. Some agonies are so severe that they ultimately result in death. Yet even in these cases, our discomfort remains temporary against the backdrop of eternity.

Drink deeply from the words of a man who knew well the agonies of suffering: "For momentary, light affliction is producing for us an eternal weight of glory far beyond all comparison, while we look not at the things which are seen, but at the things which are not seen; for the things which are seen are temporal, but the things which are not seen are eternal" (2 Corinthians 4:17–18).

In other words, all suffering will come to an end someday! Usually, we experience the unbridled joy of overcoming distress while we are still living, as the goodness of the Lord is put on vivid display. In other, more traumatic occurrences, "the sufferings of this present time are not worthy to be compared with the glory that is to be revealed to us" (Romans 8:18). Either way, we can look forward to celebrating the end of our struggles and tribulations in the future.

All Trials Can Be Productive

Regardless of the cause or duration, all trials can be remarkably productive in our lives. Because God is always working for our good in every circumstance (Romans 8:28), we can rest, knowing that a divine purpose lies behind each of our hardships. Even when our suffering is the consequence of our own actions, God graciously uses our adversity to transform us. Whether it produces deepened faith, strengthened endurance, or sincere repentance, every plight we face has a potential benefit when we respond appropriately. You may be closer to God than ever before as a result. Or you may serve God with more enthusiasm than before. Perhaps you will inspire other people through your example. Maybe your priorities will finally reflect eternity rather than the here and now. However God chooses to work in you and through you, reaping the harvest of spiritual growth is a redemptive by-product of living with the uninvited guest of heartache.

A STRANGE COMMAND

What was the worst day of your life? Did you lose a family member? Did someone you love get hurt deeply? Were you forced to battle sickness? Did the sting of betrayal or lies wreak havoc in your life? Whatever and whenever it was, you know the sinking feeling that comes when the burdens of life seem too great to bear. I want you to keep your specific example in mind as we consider what first appears to be a strange command in the book of James.

Writing to a persecuted Jewish audience dispersed around the known world, James issues what seems like an irrational, even stoic call for obedience. He simply commands, "Consider it all joy, my brethren, when you encounter various trials" (James 1:2). These words are easy to understand, but much more difficult to live. Initially, the half brother of Jesus sounds like an ivory-tower theologian with novel theories that lack the common sense required for juggling the problems of everyday life. So why should we take this instruction seriously?

Having already understood that trials can be beneficial (see chapter 5), we now move a step further in order to grasp their absolute necessity, counterintuitive as it may be. Though we work hard to avoid difficulties, the Bible presents our suffering as an integral component of our spiritual development. The resounding message of Scripture is not that God has a silver lining *if* hardships come, but that He is active and intentional *when* problems arise. In a world ravaged by sin, exposure to pain is unavoidable. Righteous Job lamented that man is born for trouble (Job 5:7) and that every person born of a woman has a brief life that is full of turmoil (Job 14:1). King David acknowledged that trouble is always near (Psalm 22:11). Despite the false hope offered by some, Christians are not exempt from the harsh realities of living. Every stage of our existence brings with it unique challenges and issues.

Resist the temptation, however, of supposing that God sits in frustration over the painful conditions we face. The Lord does much more than merely *respond to* our suffering; He sovereignly *works through* it instead. Scripture insists that many tribulations will precede our entrance into the kingdom of God (Acts 14:22). Earthly troubles are not a threat to God's plan for your life; in most cases, they are the plan! The presence of suffering is demonstrative evidence that our heavenly Father is doing the work of sanctification in our lives.

> **You cannot authentically celebrate the truth that Christ is all you need unless you are painfully aware beforehand that He is all you have.**

Trials not only change us; they also reveal who we already are. It is impossible to measure the strength of our faith apart from its being tested. You cannot, for example, fully appreciate the value of a good night's sleep without first enduring the fatigue that accompanies exhaustion. Fully valuing the refreshment a cold drink of water brings requires that we first taste the thirst that follows a day in summer's sweltering heat. Likewise, the joy of possessing faith in the Lord diminishes significantly if our commitment to Christ is never a necessity. The forerunner of standing tall for our King is, out of necessity, feeling the weight of falling to our knees. You cannot authentically celebrate the truth that Christ is all you need unless you are painfully aware beforehand that He is all you have. Without trials, our faith would remain untested and unutilized.

Your Faith Displayed

> Consider it all joy, my brethren, when you encounter various trials, *knowing that the testing of your faith* . . .
>
> *James 1:2-3 (emphasis mine)*

Despite the agony surrounding our adversities, the Bible teaches that each test of our faith serves as a confirmation that our relationship with God is real. Suffering is a fundamental means God uses to give us assurance in our faith.

Have you ever tried to verify the authenticity of a diamond? If so, you might be familiar with the heat experiment. Because real diamonds are resistant to extreme temperatures, exposing genuine stones to a flame leaves them untarnished. In addition, if you drop the same diamond into cold water after heating, its true character will be undeniable. Fake diamonds will crack and shatter due to the sudden change in temperature. A real diamond, however, will remain unaffected.

In a similar way, trials display the substance of who we are. Many who claim to have a relationship with Jesus Christ reveal the opposite reality when the harshness of a cold trial engulfs them. Real faith will shine rather than crack under pressure. To illustrate the point, Jesus told a story about two houses in His Sermon on the Mount (Matthew 7:24–27). Though they shared similar external appearances, these two structures had differing foundations under the surface. One, built by a wise man, was sturdy and strong because it rested on a rock. The other, constructed by a foolish man, was vulnerable to the elements because it towered above the sand.

When the rain fell and the wind blew, the first house stood tall while the other collapsed under its own weight. Though each home boasted a similar shape and appearance, only the former withstood the test of a storm. Likewise, those who live without the firm foundation of Jesus Christ will buckle under the pressure of severe trials. Though many people claim to love and trust God, the first signs of trouble often demonstrate otherwise. Nothing puts legitimate faith on display like adverse challenges.

Your Faith Developed

> Consider it all joy, my brethren, when you encounter various trials, knowing that the testing of your faith *produces endurance*.
>
> *James 1:2-3 (emphasis mine)*

In addition to the powerful display of genuine faith that accompanies our trials, the thorough development of our commitment is another healthy by-product of walking through difficulties. Much like a muscle lengthens and strengthens through resistance, so also our walk with Christ develops a supernatural endurance when we labor through sustained sorrow. Think of *endurance* as *perseverance*. Our capacity to persevere increases significantly each time we weather hardship without wavering in our faith. Unfortunately, repeated trials are the price we must pay to develop the fortitude we have come to associate with maturity.

Two times each year, St. Jude Hospital hosts marathons to raise funds necessary for providing world-renowned care for children who battle life-threatening cancers and diseases. Though my exercise routine has always included running short distances, I do not consider myself a natural runner. Yet, because I wanted to honor my son and bring awareness to the struggles associated with childhood cancer, I decided to register for a competition and began raising money for the hospital. Running 26.2 miles is not for the faint of heart, and I certainly did not break any records. Yet as the months of training went by, I noticed that I was able to run farther and faster with each passing week. The harder I pushed myself, the greater the results. After nearly one year of preparation, I was able to start and complete the race. My perseverance was not accidental but was the result of the repeated pain and exhaustion of running more and more each time I laced up my shoes.

Trials work the same way. Developing a spiritual toughness is impossible without experiencing the discomfort of struggles. We must learn the value and opportunity of each unbearable circumstance we face. You can *grow through* your trials or you can *wilt under* them. No wonder the apostle Paul boasted, "We also exult in our tribulations, knowing that tribulation brings about perseverance" (Romans 5:3). But why is perseverance so important?

WHO CARES ANYWAY?

We understand that trials are coming. We easily grasp that God can and does use our messes in particular ways. But why should we care? What is the end result we should hope for? Again, James provides our answer: "And let endurance have its perfect result, so that you may be perfect and complete, lacking in nothing" (James 1:4). God's target is to transform us into fully developed Christians who lack nothing. Lean hard into the hope of 1 Peter 5:10: "After you have suffered for a little while, the God of all grace, who called you to His eternal glory in Christ, will Himself perfect, confirm, strengthen and establish you." To help us see the world as He does, God beckons us to lives of maturity and wholeness. In other words, our heavenly Father is working to restore what was lost in the Garden of Eden (see chapter 1). Though the path of heartache is costly, it does not lack purpose. Becoming like our Savior is the holy ambition that drives every ounce of pain we endure. Years ago, I saved the following poem because it beautifully captures this principle:

> When God wants to drill a man,
> And thrill a man,
> And skill a man,
> When God wants to mold a man
> To play the noblest part;
> When He yearns with all His heart
> To create so great and bold a man
> That all the world shall be amazed,
> Watch His methods, watch His ways!
> How He ruthlessly perfects

Whom He royally elects!
How He hammers him and hurts him,
And with mighty blows converts him
Into trial shapes of clay which only God
    understands—
While his tortured heart is crying and he lifts
    beseeching hands!
How He bends but never breaks
When his good He undertakes . . .
How He uses whom He chooses,
And with every purpose fuses him;
By every act induces him
To try His splendor out—
God knows what He's about!

Author unknown[1]

HOW SHOULD WE RESPOND?

"Consider it all joy." What at first seemed haphazard, even cruel to our ears becomes a sweet word of encouragement when we realize the implication of these words. This command is not a heartless call to a life of seared emotions or jaded responses. Instead, God desires that we carefully and deliberately choose to rejoice by dwelling on the outcome of our sufferings. We do

---

1. Cited in Oswald Sanders, *Spiritual Leadership* (Chicago: Moody, 1978), 141. This poem appears to be a Christianized form of a poem originally written by the American poet Angela Morgan (1875–1957); see her book *Forward, March!* (New York: Lane, 1918), 92.

not enjoy trials, nor should we pretend otherwise. Smiling over open-heart surgery is just as senseless as grieving on your wedding day. Our command is to rejoice *despite* our trials, not *because* of them. Joy comes as we anticipate the result of our burdens, not from trying to ignore or diminish their severity.

Will you decide to dwell on God's outcomes rather than lamenting His methods? Choose joy today. Rest in the relentless purpose of your Savior. Yield to the powerful strength of His sovereign hand. Measure the immediate inconvenience against the future reward. Trust what you know instead of cowering to what you feel. Consider it all joy. You won't regret it.

DISCUSSION QUESTIONS

1. Do you face a sustained burden that you fear will never go away?
2. How does the temporary nature of trials change your perspective about eternity?
3. Why does the Bible teach that trials are a necessary means of spiritual growth?
4. How can you choose joy when you feel defeated or scared?

EIGHT WITH FRIENDS LIKE THESE

I sat in disbelief. Normally I don't read anonymous messages. This particular envelope, however, had "Personal" written across the front. Assuming its contents were from a friend, I opened the letter and began reading. It took my breath away.

Because Carson's weekly chemotherapy in Memphis prevented me from teaching on Wednesday evenings, this unidentified critic suggested that I was merely a part-time pastor who would be better off relocating to Tennessee. Unfortunately, this was not the worst suggestion within the contents of this hurtful correspondence. Due to this person's dissatisfaction with our church music, I read this stunning accusation:

> Since you are only a part-time pastor, we think you should get a church in Memphis and take the so-called director of music with you. Many of us have discussed his choice of music, and we don't like it (at all). Could it be true that because you didn't listen to us when we tried to discuss the music with you, God caused your child to become sick?

Really? My son had leukemia because of God's displeasure with a music style? Those words still make me cringe. How could anyone be so callous? Nothing, however, could have prepared me for what came next:

> What else will it take for you to listen to our wishes? Losing your wife, or another member of your family? You should listen to our wishes.

Against the backdrop of the previous few days, this message nearly pushed me over the edge. During our most recent visit to Memphis (week 7 out of 120), my son had a lumbar puncture in order to receive chemo in his spine. He hated being put to sleep, and the procedure was always traumatic for him. In addition, a dose of the drug Vincristine (which causes severe joint pain) and the intrusive steroid dexamethasone were also part of that week's protocol. The mood swings caused by these drugs left Heather and me fearful that Carson would not be the same after this chapter of our lives ended. Things at home were anything but encouraging, and now this.

Carson's smile helped us through the darkness.

My mind teetered between anger and anxiety. *Is this how my entire church feels? Is this view representative of the majority who gather under our roof each week?*

For the first time in my ministry, I felt like calling it quits. *If this is how God's people behave, let someone else lead them,* I reasoned. Nothing before or since has ever affected me so viscerally. I nearly buckled under the pressure.

Most of the members in that congregation were just as appalled by the letter as you might be. My family remains thankful for the many wonderful people who loved us and supported us during our time in Alabama. Our story would be incomplete, however, without acknowledging that we felt a very vocal minority working against us while Carson was ill. Nearly one-fourth of the congregation was angry because I was away each week for my son's treatment. Because this prevented me from leading our Wednesday evening activities, they felt it was an abdication of pastoral responsibility. In addition, the arrival of a new worship leader left some members angry over the kind of music we were singing in our services. A group began meeting every Tuesday while we were in Memphis to plot my dismissal from the pastorate. They mailed a letter, much of it identical to a letter they had mailed about a previous pastor, to our entire membership and called for my removal.

Forced to address the situation corporately on a Sunday morning, I simply laid my heart bare before the church. I was in no position to make demands, but I was too broken to let our grief remain under the surface. The obvious callousness at the suffering of a child and lack of empathy about my need to be with my son negated whatever legitimate concerns they might have had about my shortcomings or our church's music style, and the majority stood with us and affirmed their understanding and commitment.

When it was all over, I had the support to stay, and the disgruntled group scattered in protest. Yet the pain of the experience resulted in my asking hard questions about my future as a pastor. This dark moment left my family bewildered, wounded, and even depressed.

A PAINFUL REALITY

I chose to include these experiences because of the painful reality they highlight. Most of you will never receive a letter from an anonymous source criticizing your service to God. Thankfully, few people think this way and even fewer have the audacity to voice it to your face when they do. Some will, however, speculate to others about all the possible reasons your lifestyle might merit a trial. You might sense the not so subtle whispers behind your back that assign blame for your worst heartaches. Those who do not write you might secretly believe that whatever you are facing is exactly what you had coming. Still, the ugly underbelly of these suggestions is the belief that those who suffer the most usually earned it.

Unfortunately, even those closest *to us* will often assume the worst *about us* when a storm of difficulty arises. In fact, the people we expect to encourage us actually make our troublesome circumstances worse sometimes. Why? Though many reasons likely exist, I believe that an unbiblical view of suffering is the root cause. The average person falsely assumes that any trial or hardship must be the result of God's anger toward us. Stated simply, if people are hurting, it must be because they deserve it. Even more narcissistically, many dangerously assume that if their lives are trouble-free, it must be because they are more righteous than those who suffer.

Most will never verbalize thoughts like these, but the manifestation of our bad theology appears in multiple forms. Sometimes people are malicious and condemning rather than uplifting. Naysayers are often quick to malign their designated enemies when bad things happen to them. At other times, our self-identified supporters will subtly connect the dots between the perceived shortcomings of the wounded in an effort to propose God's immediate intentions. Seeking to have the definitive word from God, these well-intentioned friends claim to know the *what* behind every *why*. The former tear down in order to injure further, while the latter offer trite clichés in an effort to comfort. One supposes the wickedness of the wounded, while the other boasts a thorough grasp of the mind of God. Both assume, however, that repentance is the key to overcoming what ails us, resulting in an offensive sting rather than a healing balm.

These tendencies should not surprise us. Even Jesus had to push back against self-serving theology during His earthly ministry. First-century Jews assumed they could trace all suffering back to an individual's sin. Thus when encountering a man who was blind from his birth, Jesus' disciples inquired, "Who sinned, this man or his parents, that he would be born blind?" The Savior's reply was stunning: "It was neither that this man sinned, nor his parents; but it was so that the works of God might be displayed in him" (John 9:2–3). In other words, God has many purposes for our trials that are often beyond a cause-and-effect dynamic. Sin will always bring with it consequences that result in our grief, but many of the adversities we battle will have nothing to do with our previous actions.

On another occasion, tragedy struck when the tower of

Siloam fell on and killed eighteen people southeast of Jerusalem. As people inquired of Jesus about the matter, apparently their assumption was that these people were excessively wicked or else their fate would have been different. Without mincing words, Jesus replied, "Do you suppose that those eighteen on whom the tower in Siloam fell and killed them were worse culprits than all the men who live in Jerusalem? I tell you, no, but unless you repent, you will all likewise perish" (Luke 13:4–5).

Again, our Lord does not deny that sin has devastating outcomes. He does reject, however, the notion that calamities signal the excessive sinfulness and guilt of those affected. All people everywhere are sinners who need to repent, but earthly catastrophes are not an accurate measuring stick of who is in greater need of repentance. Though all heartache can be traced back to sin in general, much of our personal pain may not be caused by our particular vices.

Despite the clear teaching of Scripture, the natural inclination of our hearts is to presume the worst about those who suffer. We falsely assume that if a person faces adversity, there must be a reason for it. Thus, we surmise, those who hurt the most must deserve it. Though we may pity those in anguish, we secretly comfort ourselves that similar misfortune will never befall us as long as we keep our noses clean. The most vivid and instructive example of this egregious reasoning is found in the Old Testament narrative of Job's life. We know he suffered despite his righteousness, yet his friends absolutely refused to acknowledge such a possibility.

> **We falsely assume that if a person faces adversity, there must be a reason for it. Thus, we surmise, those who hurt the most must deserve it.**

RECOGNIZE CARELESS RESPONSES TO SUFFERING

When we survey the harsh corrections of Eliphaz, Bildad, and Zophar, we may wonder why Job considered these men friends at all. If there is any defense of their misguided rhetoric, we may at least concede that the men came to Job when he needed a friend. Not only was their desire to comfort him (Job 2:11), but they also wept over and with Job because of his condition (2:12). Perhaps their greatest gift was seven days of silence in what seemed to be an effort to provide support and empathy for God's wounded subject (2:13). Unfortunately, this is where the wisdom of Eliphaz, Bildad, and Zophar ended.

If we had time to survey the entire book of Job, we would discover three cycles of conversation between Job and his frenemies. The exchanges grow in intensity as Job responds to each man individually. In total, there are eight dialogues before a fourth friend, Elihu, enters the picture and offers a softer, albeit direct chastisement of Job. By examining the tones and content of their words, we discover repeated patterns of response that suffering individuals still face today. Recognizing these reckless attempts to show compassion will prepare us for the added stress that friends can sometimes cause, whether intentionally or accidentally.

Sarcasm That Minimizes

For reasons that are sometimes unexplainable, many who want to comfort us when life begins to unravel will minimize whatever we might be facing. Perhaps this is the result of the need that some have of measuring our calamity against their own. Or, even worse, maybe our would-be comforters are no friends at all. Regardless, some we encounter will lack the maturity and compassion necessary for refraining from insensitive remarks. Job's discourse with his counselors reveals that many of their words are barbed with sarcastic retorts and unfair rebukes.

Can you hear the dismissal as Eliphaz begins? "Should a wise man answer with windy knowledge and fill himself with the east wind? Should he argue with useless talk, or with words which are not profitable?" (Job 15:2–3). Essentially, he asserts that Job is full of hot air and lacking in wisdom. It is easy to imagine him rolling his eyes with the rhetorical question, "Were you the first man to be born, or were you brought forth before the hills? Do you hear the secret counsel of God, and limit wisdom to yourself?" (15:7–8). When speaking about the reason for Job's suffering, Eliphaz bellowed, "Is it because of your reverence that [God] reproves you, that He enters into judgment against you?" (22:4).

Bildad follows the same predictable pattern when he inquires, "How long will you say these things, and the words of your mouth be a mighty wind?" (Job 8:2). Again, the sarcastic implication is that Job is nothing more than an uninformed windbag. Zophar also embraces the destructive tactic when he questions, "Shall your boasts silence men? And shall you scoff and none rebuke?" (11:3). In other words, *You deserve what I am about to say, Job, so buckle up!*

The unifying theme of these sarcastic cracks is to diminish the legitimacy of the pain Job is feeling while depreciating any defense he offers. Likewise, you will encounter the distant cousins of these men today when trials come. Some will celebrate your anxieties because doing so makes them feel better about themselves. Others will minimize your pain in order to prop up their own anguish. Still others will seek to pull you down simply because misery loves company.

On numerous occasions, we felt the sting of those who, whether intentionally or not, minimized the scope of our family trial. "If you think this is tough, listen to what happened to me" was a common refrain. Others sometimes chided, "I know your situation is difficult, but you need to stop putting your life on hold." During one discouraging exchange, a parent whose child struggles with a life-altering disability asked how Carson was doing. While I explained his prognosis and some of the immediate challenges we faced, this mother said with obvious frustration, "You realize lots of other people are hurting too, right, and in ways far worse than what you are facing!" While I appreciate the weight this parent is carrying, it is still difficult to understand a person's need to diminish another's trial in order to magnify her own.

Accusations That Wound

Because we, like Job's friends, tend to assume the worst about those who face hardship, the frequency with which onlookers make unfounded accusations should not surprise us. Despite their predictability, these callous indictments still hurt. Consider the wounds caused by Job's brutal companions. Eliphaz blatantly insists that Job must be guilty of hidden sin against God and his fellow countrymen (Job 4:7–8; 22:5–7). "Does God pervert justice? Or does the Almighty pervert what is right?" is Bildad's way of contending for the same point (8:3). After twisting Job's words (11:4), Zophar follows with the heartless claim that though evil was like candy in Job's mouth, it became poisonous when he swallowed it (20:12–14). The bottom line here is that these men all believed that Job was getting exactly what he had coming (15:17–35).

Worse still is the backhanded notion that all of Job's children died because they were exceedingly wicked. Both Eliphaz and Bildad are less than subtle when they insinuate that the Lord punished Job's seven sons and three daughters for their rebellion (Job 4:8–9; 5:4; 8:4). Can you imagine the deep wound that this irresponsible claim caused? What provoked such cruelty? Though we cannot be certain, it is obvious that trials often become an occasion to heap long-held views and condemnation on others.

The person who secretly believes you are wicked will seldom say so when times are good, but the first sign of difficulty emboldens critics to hurl their darkest thoughts into the light. Because spectators may falsely assume that the trials of an individual vindicate their critical views of the same, their cold accusations often will follow. In our situation, we found that my son's sickness, along with the perceived weakness surrounding it, was like gasoline poured on the fiery darts of critics we did not know we had. They assured me that God only gives people what they deserve. "God is trying to *teach* you." Or "*punish* you." Or "*change* you." These were statements I heard frequently. Regardless of how self-appointed critics filled in the blank, the implication remained the same. In their view, *this* misfortune was the result of *this* deficiency in my life.

God is free to discipline us however He chooses when we sin, but our lack of knowledge about His intentions demands humility when we interact with others.

Rather than come alongside to relieve, self-appointed critics will seize on the opportunity to add weight to the heavy loads already carried by the injured.

Though the sting of being anathematized remains, one lesson I have learned through our ordeal is that the hypercritical are often hypocritical in the charges they bring. Certainly, God is free to judge and discipline us however He chooses when we sin, but our lack of knowledge about His intentions demands more humility and less presumption when we interact with others. Accusations like these are symptomatic of poor, oversimplified theology.

Theology That Oversimplifies

When perusing the remarks of Job's friends, we can clearly see how theological they sought to be. Much of their logic reveals a high view of God and a robust effort to live and think correctly. Yet the missing ingredient that derails their theology is *humility*. Much like the Pharisees who lived centuries later, these men left no room for God to work outside of their understanding. Their neatly boxed and wrapped theology was so airtight that they could not comprehend a solution different from what they offered. As a result, they frequently oversimplified the complexities of God's purposes while also offending Job in the process. For them, the premise that their friend suffered as a righteous man was not just an improbability but an impossibility.

Consider, for example, the notion that God must be angry toward us when we suffer (Job 5:1). This false dichotomy correctly allows for God to exercise His wrath when He chooses, but erroneously assumes that every burden we carry is a reflection of the Lord's hostility for our wrongdoing. In a similar way, Eliphaz's assertion that "man is born for trouble" accurately highlights the truth that every person will experience difficulties while living in a fallen world, but it egregiously assumes that we cause each problem that ails us (5:6–7).

Wrongly, Job's friends insist that there is no explanation for suffering outside of sinfulness. In their minds, no alternatives exist other than God blessing the righteous and punishing the wicked (Job 22:4). For Bildad, the entire earth would have to implode in order to allow for any other explanation (18:4). Zophar then adds that it has been this way from the beginning of time, and nothing can change it (20:4–5). Again, this perspective bears an element of truth, but it lacks the wise nuances of a more developed theology and worldview.

Though God often rewards and disciplines according to this pattern, restricting Him to predictable uniformity oversimplifies the mind of God and narrows the truth of Scripture to the point of strangling its intent. People with great integrity often endure excruciating pain (1 Thessalonians 3:3). Likewise, the wicked enjoy many of the blessings that God pours out on the earth (Matthew 5:45). Our present reality is rarely an accurate indicator of our eternal standing in the kingdom of God. To claim otherwise is grossly irresponsible. Tragically, many would-be theologians use God as a weapon to win their arguments rather than pointing to Him as the Lord who is there as our ever-present help during times of trouble (Psalm 46:1). Repeatedly throughout Carson's illness, we endured misguided calls for repentance, appeals for more faith, and arrogant declarations of *all* that God desired to accomplish in our lives.

Theology really does matter.

Solutions That Are Misapplied

Bad theology inevitably leads to trite misapplications of truth. Convinced that his views on suffering were impenetrable, Eliphaz dangerously elevated his experience as an authority in Job's life. Apparently, his interpretation of a recent dream convinced him that his hurting friend was guilty and in need of repentance (Job 4:12–16). Beware of any person who has a message *from God* that is outside of Scripture and is specifically *for you*. Errors like these are still quite common.

A few years ago, a friend of mine had an exhausting battle with chronic headaches and sinus issues. Though he and his wife did not know the concerned believer who paid them a visit in their home, they were appreciative that she was willing to come and pray for his relief. Shortly after arriving, however, the woman explained that she had a dream of Jesus holding and petting a lamb, and in her view, my friend was that lamb. To her it was a sign of God's eagerness to heal. Three times she placed her hands on my friend's head in order to intercede on his behalf. At the conclusion of each prayer, she stopped to ask how he felt. Her obvious frustration grew when he admitted the pain was still there. Exasperated by the inactivity, the woman proceeded to question the husband and wife about immorality in their lives, suggesting that the sin of adultery was preventing miraculous healing. Like Job's friends, she understood sin's devastating consequences but applied them to the wrong person, causing more offense than comfort.

Similarly, Bildad's insistence that God was punishing Job also grew out of a misguided effort to apply what was true. Despite correctly asserting the Lord's sovereignty over all the earth, he dangerously concluded that Job, along with any other wounded person, could not, in light of his severe trials, be righteous (Job 25:1–6). The God who controls all things would not, Bildad reasoned, allow such harsh circumstances to unfold in the life of anyone who was fully committed to Him. Thus Job could not possibly be righteous, and repentance was the only solution.

Elihu, Job's fourth friend who emerges late in the narrative, repeats the same blunder even while extolling God's providential reign over all things (Job 33). In this particular instance, the rule of God was not a witness against the integrity of Job. His friends continually declared half-truths that were not relevant to Job.

Threats That Frighten

Almost without fail, those who view themselves as authorities over the events unfolding in your life will resort to apocalyptic threats intended to warn you about the future. In his effort to persuade Job, Eliphaz chided, "Snares surround you, and sudden dread terrifies you, or darkness, so that you cannot see, and an abundance of water covers you" (Job 22:10–11). Next he countered with a question, "Will you keep to the ancient path which wicked men have trod, who were snatched away before their time, whose foundations were washed away by a river?" (22:15–16). In a similar way, Bildad graphically accosted his friend by describing the path of the wicked as a binding trap that consumes strength, devours skin, and tears away security (18:11–15). We encounter the same tactic from Zophar as he attempts to bully Job with the strength of God (11:7–11), followed by a grim picture of God's fierce judgment on the wicked (20:23–29).

Much like the writer of the anonymous letter I received, some people will be quick to provide instructions for avoiding even greater grief in order to chronicle the consequences if you do not listen. Some do so vindictively, while others are more altruistic. In either instance, however, the implication is that a personal shortcoming caused your trial, and therefore you must choose a different course. In my case, it was "change the church music or lose your wife." For you, it may be more genteel, but frequently there will be calls to alter your lifestyle in order to avoid future trials. Though God often convicts and transforms us during times like these, we should not feel pressured to yield to every warning we receive from passive observers gathered around us.

Clichés That Insult

While some people mistreat the wounded due to their bad theology, others would just as soon avoid theology altogether. No one enjoys worn-out and meaningless pep talks that are oblivious to the agony of the moment, yet modern Christianity has an abundance of shallow one-liners. As you might expect, cotton candy comfort is nothing new. Eliphaz instructs Job to "seek God" and place his cause before Him because of the guaranteed results that would be sure to follow (Job 5:8). Despite the fact that Job continually seeks the Lord throughout the heated exchange with his friends, do you sense how insulting the simplicity of this advice is against the gravity of his predicament?

Modern equivalents include, "Just trust God!" "He has a plan!" "God is good all the time!" and "The best is yet to come!" For someone who's walking through the fire, statements like these are insensitive and insulting. Hearing others promise what they do not know, as if their greeting card counsel conveys some sort of fresh revelation, is beyond annoying. If I had a nickel for every time someone assured me of their thoughts and prayers, I would be a wealthy man. To me, this approach signaled a lack of genuine concern for our situation and a confession that these individuals would never think about Carson again, much less earnestly pray for him.

Bildad's retort is more of the same, telling Job in effect that if he would only beg for the compassion of God, his end would be far better than his beginning (Job 8:5–7). In other words, *God's got this, Job! Just relax, humble yourself, and watch God work.* Zophar follows suit with some false optimism of his own. If he were around today, he would have pleaded, "Just behave appropriately, Job, and make sure God is in your heart" (11:13–14). *Everything will be fine*, in other words, *if you just follow the formula and complete steps 1 through 3. If you have a problem, just play the game and God will fix it.* Again, tired admonishments like these do very little to comfort those who are hurting, and even worse, they imply a deficiency of commitment that likely caused the current plight. What could be more insulting than offering someone advice that you have never needed and, consequently, was born out of an experience that you did not have?

THE BIG TAKEAWAY

Without question, the number of people who lined up to encourage and support us during Carson's war with cancer far exceeded the number of those who added to our distress. Close friends from Chattanooga came to the hospital and delivered gifts, cards, and well-wishes from our previous congregation. Our favorite photographer, knowing we would miss out otherwise, drove hundreds of miles to Memphis to capture our son Brady's first birthday. Members of churches from all over Memphis visited us, prayed for us, and tangibly encouraged us. One pastor provided us with an apartment free of charge so our family could come to visit Carson whenever they liked; another loaned me his car to use as much as we needed, and many of these same men invited me to share with their congregations what God was teaching us.

People from all over the world wrote us and lifted us up to God on Carson's behalf. These remarkable demonstrations of love within the body of Christ breathed life into our hurting souls.

Yet the depression caused by a few was real and daunting. In the spirit of remaining positive, people seldom talk honestly about the meaningless pain that well-intended friends and closet enemies often cause during tough times. Our story, however, would be incomplete without acknowledging that many of our anxieties were entirely unnecessary.

My prayer is that these insights will help you understand the troubling behavior of some who might be close to you. Even more, my hope is that the yoke of adversity will be a bit lighter because you are better prepared when you experience responses similar to what Job heard. Focus on those who love and comfort you. Be patient with those who want to help but unintentionally fall short of what they intend. Ignore those who seek to do you harm. No matter what, remember that God will have the last word on your suffering.

DISCUSSION QUESTIONS

1. What is most offensive about the anonymous letter the author received?
2. How can bad theology result in your hurting someone else?
3. Have you ever been wounded by the careless words of another while you were suffering?
4. Which of the errors listed in the chapter is most common today?
5. How should you respond to those who speak to you carelessly?

NINE

THE MOST COURAGEOUS FAITH

Working our way through the Memphis airport was now as customary to Carson and me as sitting down at the dinner table. After passing through security, we often visited our favorite bookstore inside the terminal, followed by a quick snack before boarding a plane to Atlanta. Routine was important to us because each step felt like progress. As we walked down the hallway lined by brown brick walls, a young man we did not know approached us. His eyes were full of kindness, and it was obvious he wanted to speak to Carson. After greeting me, the mutual traveler dropped to one knee while asking for permission to pray for my son. Of course, I was happy to indulge him because we were now very accustomed to the power of prayer on Carson's behalf.

I do not remember his exact words, but I do recall the urgency of this man's petition for an immediate miracle. He asked God to heal Carson, to increase our faith, and to make future doctor visits unnecessary. After finishing, he stood to his feet and declared that Carson was healed and that everything would be fine from that point forward. His prescription for the future was to trust God and leave our trips to St. Jude behind us. Faith was the key to unlock all that he was claiming for my son.

Left speechless by his comments, I could not say a word until after the man walked away. I was all too familiar with prosperity theology, which presupposes that all problems can be avoided, all visions can be funded, and all sicknesses can be healed. Before, it was just another category of theological malpractice. Now, with my son fighting for his life, the predictable, unbiblical message of speaking your reality into existence was deeply offensive. My surprise over the incident quickly gave way to anger. For months, Heather and I walked with our son through this ordeal, praying for him, trusting God to heal him, and rearranging our entire lives to make it a reality. How could a stranger dare insinuate that if we just believed God more, Carson would have already been healed? Here was a person with nothing invested, who did not even know our names, who positioned himself as the channel of a blessing that we were too ignorant or negligent to claim. How insulting!

Thankfully, Carson was so young at this point that he understood very little about what happened. To him, this prayer was no different from the hundreds of others he heard previously when friends came to check on him. Yet the events of that day forced me to reexamine my understanding of faith as I tried to understand more fully what it means to trust God. I, too, believed that God was going to heal Carson, but only

The most courageous faith trusts God in order to endure a hardship that is present.

after he completed his leukemia treatment protocol. In fact, the conviction was so strong as I prayed that I stopped asking God for an instantaneous miracle and began pleading for endurance instead. *Am I wrong? Did I miss something in seminary? Are miracles ours for the taking? Do all sicknesses have to flee if we believe sincerely enough? Has my lack of faith somehow prevented what God wants to do in my son's life?*

Let me make it more personal. *Can you overcome any illnesses you face? Do you have to remain in a wheelchair? Should you stop chemotherapy to fight your cancer? Is the use of medication an indication that you lack faith in God? Can you claim healing for your family member or friend who is suffering?* Questions like these drove me to search the Scriptures for answers. In doing so, I experienced a renewed conviction about God's healing power while rejecting the damaging and misleading claims of faith healers.

Eyeing the chemotherapy finish line

The most courageous faith does not believe in order to claim a miracle that is absent, but instead trusts God in order to endure a hardship that is present. Believing what God *can do* requires less faith than walking with the Lord despite what He *refuses to do.* The former is a test of His power; the latter is a test of His heart. Certainly the confidence to trust God for healing is important, but the contentment to trust Him when sickness remains is even more so.

GOOD COMPANY

The notion that the presence of illness indicates a lack of faith on the part of those who suffer or those who love them is easily debunked. Consider the circumstances surrounding some of the Bible's most faithful characters. Not only did Paul battle a persistent thorn in his flesh (most believe it was an eyesight problem) with no relief, but he also watched helplessly as his closest allies endured physical challenges as well. Trophimus remained sick in Miletus despite the missionary's time there (2 Timothy 4:20). Timothy, the apostle's protégé in the ministry, battled stomach issues and frequent ailments. The only recourse was mixing a bit of wine with his water for relief (1 Timothy 5:23).

Can you imagine chastising these men for their unbelief? Few, if any, will ever be as faithful in taking the gospel to others as these servants of God. Yet if we follow contemporary charismatic logic, the substance of their faith was deficient because they lacked definitive healing. The premise would be laughable if the stakes were not so high. Nothing is more deflating than implying that the exhausted commitment and belief of hurting saints lacked the silver bullet necessary for putting their ailment to death. Having watched parents plead with God on behalf of their children, only to have their hearts torn apart by despair and their cheeks stained with tears, I cannot imagine insisting that it all could have been avoided if their faith had been more real.

Amazingly, the man in the airport was not my final encounter with misinformed healing rhetoric. A familiar grimace furled my brow when I opened an envelope containing a letter and book from a concerned woman in another state. Though I shrugged off her letter as misguided sincerity, I still shook my head in frustration after reading her instructions:

You don't need a doctor to heal your son.
Read this book and do everything it says.

Just have faith and everything will be fine.
Claim Carson's healing from the Lord.

Really? Is it *really* that simple? Are the multitudes of people in hospitals around the world only there because they failed to follow a superstitious formula? What if a person never discovers the *magic* book I received? Does God withhold His goodness if we recite a prayer incorrectly or get a list out of order? Ideas like these are not only nonsensical; they are damaging.

PART OF THE PLAN?

Though God is not the cause of disease and illness, it should comfort us to know that He is always in control of our physical infirmities. Nothing comes across the pages of your life without God's permission and design. Jesus reassures us, "Are not two sparrows sold for a cent? And yet not one of them will fall to the ground apart from your Father. But the very hairs of your head are all numbered. So do not fear; you are more valuable than many sparrows" (Matthew 10:29–31). If this is true, why does God allow sickness to plague us?

A Greater Good

God chooses the path of illness at times to serve a greater good. The manifest glory of God and the eternal good of humanity govern every trial we face. Even when the divine ambition is the glory of Christ, every difficulty works for our good as well. Though God does not cause our suffering and pain, He is sovereign over it. Comprehending the ways in which the Lord works within and through every diagnosis we receive is mind-boggling, but the fact that He does is true nonetheless. His judgments are unsearchable, and His actions are unfathomable (Romans 11:33).

Consequences for Our Actions

While we should reject a paranoia that suspects every illness is the direct result of sin, we cannot dismiss the reality that sinful actions bring heartache and devastating consequences. Sickness is *not always* a natural result of an individual's sin, but because we are physical beings, our choices certainly can affect our bodies. Tobacco use can cause cancer. Overeating may result in diabetes. Sexual promiscuity increases the risk of contracting sexually transmitted diseases. Lack of exercise and a poor diet can diminish our overall health. Tracing many of the ailments we suffer back to our behaviors is not difficult. Such maladies are not due to a lack of faith at the moment of diagnosis but are the result of our previous choices instead.

Neither should we discount that the Lord sometimes causes our decline in health due to our wicked behavior and fleshly attitudes. For Christians, actions like these are redemptive rather than punitive. God lovingly corrects rather than angrily punishing His own. Still, the Lord is not idle when believers choose to sin, and physical sickness is His chosen response at times.

The Bible warns, for example, that a refusal to examine yourself when coming to the Lord's Supper can result in illness or even death (1 Corinthians 11:30). When the Old Testament king Uzziah rebelled against the law's priestly order by entering the temple to burn incense, God immediately struck him with leprosy as a result (2 Chronicles 26:19–20). Ananias's and

Sapphira's willingness to lie to the Holy Spirit ended with their falling dead before the Jerusalem church (Acts 5:1–11). In these instances, the correlation between sinful conduct and physical consequences is undeniable.

Connections like these are not always so clear today, but they are possible. The Lord's discipline is a loving exercise designed to bring us back into fellowship with Him and into deeper holiness (Hebrews 12:9–10). The sober message of Scripture is that God will use any means possible to correct His wayward people:

> You have not yet resisted to the point of shedding blood
> in your striving against sin; and you have forgotten the
> exhortation which is addressed to you as sons,
>
> "My son, do not regard lightly the discipline of
> the Lord,
> nor faint when you are reproved by Him;
> for those whom the Lord loves He disciplines,
> and He scourges every son whom He receives."
>
> *Hebrews 12:4–6*

Again, the emphasis here is on God's willingness to help us resist sin at any cost. No one enjoys sickness or the grief it causes, yet many will testify to the "peaceful fruit of righteousness" that results from its presence (Hebrews 12:11). The psalmist is more direct in his assessment of these outcomes: "Before I was afflicted I went astray, but now I keep Your word" (Psalm 119:67). When physical trauma or weakness is the manifested consequence of our bad behavior, we would do well to repent of our sins and return to the Lord.

A Spiritual Attack

In addition to what we can control, we also have an archenemy who is anxious to exploit our physical weaknesses. As a result, sickness can at times be the direct result of Satan's efforts. Much like Job's undeserved affliction, the devil may initiate our physical pain and uncertainty to undermine our trust in the Lord. With the ultimate goal of proving that God is only glorious because of *what* He does for us rather than simply because of *who* He is, Eden's serpent chides us to curse God instead of follow Him.

When describing the ministry of Jesus, Peter acknowledged the sinister activity of Satan as it sometimes relates to sickness: "You know of Jesus of Nazareth, how God anointed Him with the Holy Spirit and with power, and how He went about doing good and healing all who were oppressed by the devil, for God was with Him" (Acts 10:38). Apparently, the efforts of the wicked one were the root cause of many afflictions Jesus chose to heal. On one occasion, Jesus cast a demon out of a son whom the Bible describes as a "lunatic" who was "very ill" (Matthew 17:14–18). While teaching in the synagogue on the Sabbath, our Savior encountered a woman who "had a sickness caused by a spirit" (Luke 13:11). For reasons that are not always clear and purposes that we cannot usually fathom, God allows and uses attacks like these in the battle for His kingdom.

WHAT IS THE PRAYER OF FAITH?

If my characterization of those who manipulate faith for their own advantage is true, clarifying one important passage of Scripture is essential. While writing about those who are sick (literally, "without strength"), the half brother of Jesus commends:

> Is anyone among you sick? Then he must call for the elders of the church and they are to pray over him, anointing him with oil in the name of the Lord; and the prayer offered in faith will restore the one who is sick, and the Lord will raise him up, and if he has committed sins, they will be forgiven him.
>
> *James 5:14–15*

The overall tone and message of these verses make it clear that God is not only able but also willing to heal at times. My criticisms of those who claim signs and wonders as if they are door prizes should not be interpreted as a rejection of God's supernatural power. To the contrary, Scripture is unambiguous that Jesus readily healed, His disciples did the same, and God the Father frequently chooses to follow suit when we pray. But as we have seen, the will of God is multifaceted, and purposes beyond our immediate understanding sometimes result in His refusal to give us what we so desperately plead for. God can heal, but He does not always deem it best to do so.

Next, we should recognize that it is the responsibility of the person who is ill to call for the elders of the church. Contrary to what we often observe on television, self-appointed faith healers should not walk around looking for someone to heal. The prayer for this individual takes place in the privacy of a home, not in a worship service designed for the healing of the multitudes. Because God does not choose to heal every person's physical infirmity, claiming miracles for the masses in large gatherings fueled by the hope and desperation of the audience seems counterproductive. When the primary goal of worship is the eradication of our burdens—in this case, sickness—failing to hit the target leaves individuals feeling devastated and rejected by God.

Instead, saints should gather corporately in order to give themselves more fully to the Lord rather than to get something from Him. Granted, our Savior often blesses us beyond our greatest expectation or imagination, and we rightly praise Him when He does. Yet making ourselves—and, in this instance, our need—the driving focus of a corporate gathering is more akin to self-indulgence than biblical worship. Most healing services result in the majority feeling *snubbed* by Christ the Son rather than *strengthened* by Him, precisely because He was never our focus in the first place.

We must also appreciate that God does not require a donation before a miracle can occur. Simply following the money trail exposes the true agenda of many false teachers. Jesus never put a price tag on His work, because the healing we long for is not for sale. In fact, the Bible reserves one of its sharper rebukes for a man named Simon, a sorcerer who sought to purchase the power of God after he observed the ministry of the apostles (Acts 8:18–23). The notion of a *seed offering*, popularized by certain movements, is completely foreign to the Bible. Reaping a miracle is never promised just because we sowed the seed of dollars and cents.

In fact, Scripture identifies ideas like these as heretical religion, doing great damage to the cause of Christ (2 Peter 2:1–2). When speaking about false prophets, the apostle Peter warned, "In their greed they will exploit you with false words; their judgment from long ago is not idle, and their destruction is not asleep" (2:3). Those who prey on the vulnerable anxieties of others with promises they cannot keep will answer to God. In the meantime, we should aggressively reject such dangerous teaching.

So what exactly should take place when the leaders of the church gather around individuals in order to seek their healing? Two ingredients leap off the page of James's instruction. Praying over patients and anointing them with oil are the two means God uses to reveal His intentions (James 5:14). Certainly, standing over a patient's bed to pray would fit the description here, but I believe James is referring to more than our physical posture and bedside manner. To "pray over" is to seek and discern the will of God about the matter at hand. By asking God if He desires to heal, the elders can gauge whether to pray for healing or comfort. The "prayer offered in faith" cannot be manipulated simply because of our desires. To the contrary, God initiates the faith that those who pray are to offer back to Him. In other words, the Lord grants the faith by which we pray.

Thus, the text does not assure us that a sick believer *might* be made well but that he *will* be restored to health (James 5:15). Our understanding of this guarantee must rest in God's willingness to reveal His desire and our cooperation to pray in faith as He directs. We are not free to impose our predetermined outcome and then hold God accountable for our decision. Instead, we pursue His direction, and we yield to it as we intercede.

Anointing with oil also supports the idea of uncovering and submitting to the will of God. Though many correctly insist that oil served medicinal purposes in the first century, its healing impact would have been minimal in light of the severe illness described by the text. Consequently, perceiving this lubricant as a symbol of our surrender to the Holy Spirit is the best interpretation. James intended the outward presence of oil to signify a person's inward dedication to God's work. Just as Moses anointed the high priest, his utensils, the altar, and the tabernacle itself with oil in order to consecrate them to the Lord (Leviticus 8:10–12), doing the same for homebound Christians is a declaration of our intent to accept God's plan for them. In this sense, physical maladies may lead to spiritual healing, no matter their outcome.

No wonder James concludes his admonishment with this: "if he has committed sins, they will be forgiven him" (James 5:15). Yielding to God's agenda will result in either God granting faith that leads to our healing or, something even more spectacular, God granting faith to endure in pain for the sake of eternal reward.

Forever etched in my memory is an adorable young girl with an intrusive drainage tube running down and out the side of her head because of a recent brain surgery. I readily recall a handsome little boy, not much older than Carson, who could barely walk down the hallways of St. Jude following the aggressive amounts of radiation he received. When I close my eyes at night, sometimes I see a small child with only one beautiful eye staring back at me after he lost the other due to retinoblastoma.

These precious children did not deserve to fight childhood cancer, and their parents were not negligent because they did. God did not begrudgingly withhold their miracle after selling out to the highest bidder. Faith was not absent; it was evident in every earnest prayer offered by their families. The mere suggestion that the conditions of these babies were the result of deficient faith or money that was never sown is more than an insult; it is a hellish lie.

DISCUSSION QUESTIONS

1. Has anyone ever questioned your faith because of a miracle they perceived to be unclaimed in your life?
2. In your view, what is the greatest expression of genuine faith?
3. Does God always give us the miracles we ask Him for? Why or why not?
4. What is the difference between a trial and a consequence?
5. How should we understand the prayer of faith?

TEN THE ANSWERS YOU WEREN'T LOOKING FOR

I almost dropped my phone. After tucking Carson into bed on one of our weekly trips to Memphis, I read through the day's emails, as was my custom. Just one month shy of the one-year anniversary of his diagnosis, Carson now had less than two years of chemotherapy remaining. Slowly his hair had begun to regrow, and along with it, our optimism that cancer could soon be in our rearview mirror.

The Wright family had been part of our journey from the beginning. Their beautiful daughter, Logan, was battling lymphoma. They lived just down the hall when we were staying at the Ronald McDonald House. After they began attending our Sunday morning worship time in the chapel, our relationship grew into one of mutual respect and encouragement. Carson and Logan frequently played together within the safe, germ-free parameters we created in the common areas of our temporary home.

By now, both of our families were well into the protocols prescribed for our kids. Though we did not see one another as often, our interactions in waiting rooms and the Memphis

Grizzlies House (since renamed the Tri Delta Place) at St. Jude were still common.

Unprepared for what I was about to read, I gasped for air as my eyes stumbled over the words, *Logan passed away on Friday.* Apparently, a severe fungal infection in her lungs did not respond to antibiotics, requiring surgery to clean them out. While under anesthesia, Logan's heart just stopped. For weeks, all I could see when I closed my eyes was her radiating smile. Her personality lit up every room, and I could not imagine the world without her. A few days later, I spoke at her funeral.

The short life of our dear friend Logan inspires countless families.

The impact of Logan's death was far-reaching. In addition to the deep wound seared into the hearts of her loved ones, many St. Jude friends were left struggling to face similar possibilities with their own children. For Heather and me, the fear was palpable. Logan was more than a face we saw in a hallway occasionally. We knew these people, and despite our growing confidence, now we were not as certain that Carson would beat leukemia. *Why did their daughter have to die while our son continues to live? Is it naive to believe our son has a future? How could God allow such a terrible thing to happen?*

NEVER POSITIONED
TO CORRECT GOD

Returning to the familiar story of Job reminds us again that asking God why bad things happen is always permissible. The Lord invites us to bring our troubles to Him, and we should never be afraid to do so (Matthew 11:28–30). Job's desire to understand, however, slowly transformed into an eagerness to correct his Maker, despite his inability to do so. Using the image of a courtroom, he acknowledges that no mortal is in a position to argue with God. Speaking of the Lord, Job lamented, "If one wished to dispute with Him, he could not answer Him once in a thousand times" (Job 9:3).

And therein lies the problem. Deep down, we realize we cannot challenge any of God's judgments, yet we are eager to try nonetheless. *Why this, Lord?* is a desperate plea for comfort and wisdom as we stare down life's most egregious circumstances. But *What are You doing, Lord?* is a painful accusation that God's decisions lack sound reasoning and compassion. The former seeks the strength and intervention of our Creator, while the latter implies that He is not qualified, at least in our case, to render the verdict He chose.

Though Job never questioned God's power to act however He chooses, neither did he conclude that God is always right in what He does. Despite his inability to fathom the mind of God, Job still questioned the legitimacy of God's behavior toward him (Job 9:10–12). In other words, he was not only puzzled about God's *conduct*; he was disappointed in *who* he perceived God to be. Sadly, Job portrayed the Lord as a cruel bully before whom there is no defense. Listen to the pain in his words:

"For He bruises me with a tempest
And multiplies my wounds without cause.
He will not allow me to get my breath,
But saturates me with bitterness.
If it is a matter of power, behold, He is the strong one!
And if it is a matter of justice, who can summon Him?
Though I am righteous, my mouth will condemn me;
Though I am guiltless, He will declare me guilty."

Job 9:17–20

Thus, rather than lean hard into God's goodness for comfort, Job, in this instance, ran from Him in hopelessness. At other moments, we see the same wounded man ascend to the highest point of faith's mountain in order to rest completely in God's sovereignty over His life (Job 19:25–26). But these scenes are not monolithic. Oftentimes, we observe Job struggling one minute and rejoicing the next. In another scene, he longs to have an audience with God while agonizing that God is nowhere to be found (23:2–3). Then a few verses later, he seems to rejoice in great hope: "[God] knows the way I take; when He has tried me, I shall come forth as gold" (23:10).

Do we not follow the same pattern? One moment we wrestle with God in the depths of despair, and the next we cry out in tremendous determination and praise. Throughout Carson's treatment, we continually cycled between crippling weariness and undeterred devotion, sometimes in the same day. When our friend Logan died, the rhythmic victory we were enjoying seemed to pass with her. With the wind out of our sails, our dreams of having a healthy son suddenly felt like wishful thinking.

This was not the first time we battled doubt. Even before Logan's passing, the devastating outcomes of cancer became real to us. The Tolletts quickly and easily became our friends shortly after our arrival at St. Jude because of their strong Christian faith. Their four-year-old son, Justin, was battling a deadly medullo-blastoma tumor at the base of his

> One moment we wrestle with God in the depths of despair, and the next we cry out in tremendous determination and praise.

brain. Despite encouraging signs early on in his treatment, Justin's surgeries, radiation, and chemotherapy ravaged his young body with side effects. Watching him struggle was painful, and when the news of his death came, the same debilitating fear taunted us.

Clouded by our incessant questions about God's motive in these sad outcomes, we found that being strong for our son was increasingly difficult for a season. We teetered between resting in God's perfect plan and wondering if the Lord knew what He was doing. Like Job, I longed for the opportunity to present my airtight logic for why these harsh circumstances should not be unfolding. In my mind,

> "I would present my case before Him
> And fill my mouth with arguments.
> I would learn the words which He would answer,
> And perceive what He would say to me.
> Would He contend with me by the greatness of
> His power?
> No, surely He would pay attention to me.
> There the upright would reason with Him;
> And I would be delivered forever from my Judge."
>
> *Job 23:4–7*

Though I am ashamed to admit how deeply my faith was lacking at points in Carson's journey, I am grateful for the Lord's patience with me, as well as His willingness to teach me about Himself. It was through these stints of sorrow that I tested my belief in God's right to have the final authority over everything that happens to my family. So many of my questions were never answered, but by examining how God responded to Job, I realized the significant flaws in my reasoning.

THE REAL ANSWER TO OUR DEEPEST HURTS

Have you ever noticed how we are much more open to the Lord in the midst of our personal chaos and disruption? If for no other reason, trials are beneficial because they force us into a posture of longing to hear God's voice. After the lengthy debate between Job and his friends, God speaks to His bludgeoned son out of a whirlwind (Job 38:1). His answer is not at all what we expect: "Who is this that darkens counsel by words without knowledge?" (38:2). Translation: *Who are you to speak such foolishness to Me, Job?* Hardly the compassionate solace we expected for a man who was hurting so severely. The Lord is even more aggressive with His corrective gaze as He continues: "Now gird up your loins like a man, and I will ask you, and you instruct Me!" (38:3). Job wanted to put God on the witness stand, but he soon became the defendant in heaven's courtroom.

While God's responses are not gentle, the relentless nature of His inquiries is instructive. Keep in mind that Job never rebelled against his Maker, though he suffered greatly, and he refused to curse God, despite the promptings of those closest to him. He did, however, call God's judgment into question as he tried to process the hardship in his life. The answer he received from the Lord, though shocking, is more comforting than he, and we, could ever imagine.

And how does God answer Job? Not with a series of explanations, but with a list of questions of His own. First, He uses creation to illustrate who holds authority over the whole earth. Allow me to paraphrase the divine interrogation (Job 38–39):

> Where were you when I laid the foundation of
> the earth, Job?
> Did you measure its parameters?
> Did you establish its foundations?
> Did you hear the angels worship as I worked?
> Were you there when I set the boundaries for the sea?
> Do you command the light to illuminate each day?
> Have you been to the bottom of the ocean?
> Do you have any idea how big My creation is?
> Do you know where I store the snow and hail?
> Or how I make them fall?
> Who guides the wind, the flood, and the thunderbolt?
> Can you make it rain?
> Can you throw lightning on the earth?
> Can you number the clouds and release their water?
> Can you turn dust into mud?
> How do you explain the constellations?
> Can you feed the lions? Or the ravens?
> Do you help the goats and deer birth their young?
> And care for them afterward?

Do you know who sets wild donkeys free?

Can you tame wild oxen?

Who makes the ostrich dumb and fast?

Do you give a horse its strength? Or mane? Or speed?
    Or courage?

Do you cause the hawk to soar?

Did you teach the eagle to build his nest in high places?

Feeling small yet? Do you see the point? We are never in a position to correct God—no matter how painful, tragic, or devastating life becomes—because *He is God*, and we are not. Strangely, this is more comforting than we expect it to be. Instead of providing answers to the particular questions we wrestle with, God reminds us that, though His ways are not our ways, He has quite a track record of ruling over the universe. The assurance here is *not* that He allows us to understand the eternal method behind our momentary madness, but that He is more than capable of handling it. Why? *Because having God with us is better than any explanation He might offer.* The freedom that comes from letting go is not a sign that our burdens do not matter but that we could never comprehend the full scope of what God is doing in our lives.

Still not convinced? Allow our Creator's final words to Job to resonate within your heart: "Will the faultfinder contend with the Almighty? Let him who reproves God answer it" (Job 40:2). In other words, *Did you have something to say? Do My actions not meet with your approval?* Chances are that Job felt just like we do in similar situations. Feel the comforting humility of his response: "Behold, I am insignificant; what can I reply to You? I lay my hand on my mouth. Once I have spoken, and I will not answer; even twice, and I will add nothing more" (40:4–5).

Yet God is not finished, lest we drift back toward a moral authority that is not ours to wield. In a second series of questions, the Lord connects the ethical dots for us to navigate our troubles better. He begins, "Will you really annul My judgment? Will you condemn Me that you may be justified?" (Job 40:8). These two questions capture the essence of why our insights will never rival God's.

> The freedom that comes from letting go is not a sign that our burdens do not matter but that we could never comprehend the full scope of what God is doing in our lives.

Do we really feel more qualified than God to make decisions?

Would we rather have God seem unfair so that we might look and feel better?

Do we really want to diminish God just to create an explanation for our suffering?

As harsh and confusing as life can be, the price for calling God's character into question is much greater than we want to pay.

Next, God invites Job, and us, to sit on His throne in order to execute our wisdom over living creatures (Job 40:9–14). Then with two examples from the animal kingdom, God again humbles us with the reminder of our inability to contend with creation, much less our Creator (40:15–23; 41:1–34). If what God made frightens us, how much more should the Lord Himself cause us to tremble? Who are we to correct or counsel Him?

OUR BOTTOM LINE

I was numb while driving from Alabama to Louisiana for Logan's funeral. I still could not believe she was gone and that the Wrights were burying their daughter. Speaking at the funeral was unlike any ministerial assignment before or since, because all I could think about was what I would think and feel if Carson were in that tiny casket. Nothing could have prepared me, though, for the wave of emotion that engulfed me when I saw our precious friend lying there. She looked so peaceful, and yet very much gone. All I could see was my son in that box, and I could not hold back the tears. I prayed while we sang, begging God to give me the right words to share.

It was almost too much to bear. Then I looked over to the front row at Logan's parents as they grieved. In the clarity of that moment, God reminded me of something. Her parents, Russell and LaTonya, were relatively new Christians who had recommitted their lives to Christ after one of the services we shared at the Ronald McDonald House. I watched in amazement as the two of them lifted their hands to heaven, and though they were distressed, they worshiped the Lord. Rooted in their faith, they possessed a strong confidence that they would see their daughter again.

What if Logan had never had cancer? Certainly, she would still be alive today. But what if, in the goodness and sovereignty of God, her sickness was the chosen instrument that brought her parents back to the Lord? Or what if Logan's life touched an anonymous bystander who turned to Christ as a result? These possibilities cannot be proven, but I'm simply illustrating that God works in mysterious ways. At times, God bruises us before He comforts us. In other instances, the only way to help us in the end is to hurt us in the present. Unfortunately, we are not always sure *what* God is doing, but we can still trust *who* God is. On that difficult day, I found great peace knowing that the Lord is strong and kind, even when those attributes are less clear to me.

Lessons like these do not come cheap. Usually, we learn them on the anvil of adversity when much is at stake. So what should we remember the next time we begin to doubt God's decisions about our lives? The following fundamental truths function like anchors that keep me steadied when the wind blows.

- **Questions about God's activity in your life are permissible.** The Lord did not rebuke Job because he cried out to Him for answers. Demanding answers and chastising God when they do not come, however, crosses a line. Be careful to resist the temptation to impugn God's motives or diminish His integrity. The freedom to bring our confusion to the Lord is not a license to sit in judgment of Him.
- **Knowing God is far better than understanding His plans for you.** Remember, a single explanation about your current trials will leave you anxious and afraid when a new hardship arises. But if you appreciate and trust the character of God, you will not feel helpless, even when life unravels. Sometimes God graciously does not tell us what we will face or how long we must endure it. Your lack of answers may be the heavenly Father's protective measure rather than an attempt to frustrate you.
- **What we want is not always what we need.** Job did not expect the response God gave him, but it was exactly what he needed from the Lord. As hard as it is to grasp, many of our worst days are absolutely necessary for God's eternal outcomes to become a reality for us. Nothing deepens our intimacy with and our wonder of God like yielding to Him when it is difficult to do so.

Jerry and Kristie Tollett demonstrated a remarkable reliance on the Lord when their son Justin died. Theirs is not a story of supernatural insight or minimal struggle. To the contrary, accepting God's will has been difficult for them, and many of their questions remain unanswered. Amazingly, these heartbroken parents surrender again and again to God's incomprehensible course in their lives. I first read of Justin's death on a Sunday morning, January 29, just ten months after his initial diagnosis. His mother's words that day inspired me, and they still do today. On a blog to keep friends and loved ones informed about Justin's condition, she wrote:

> I don't know why this is God's will, and I am almost positive I don't want to know. I believe in God and I know that His end plan is greater than my comprehension . . . [One possibility is that] his dad and I will know without a doubt that Justin is in heaven. He will never be tempted by so many sins. He will never take the first drink, or drug. Bad words will never exit his mouth. His life as an adult will never bring disgrace to his parents or to God. So many things we as adults will have to answer God for will never be on his heart. I would rather have a four-year-old son in heaven than an eighty-year-old son in hell.

Unbelievable. I pray God will give me that kind of faith and courage, no matter what my future holds. Again, we do not know the breadth of why God chose to take Justin to heaven. Yet this mother's remarkable insight is instructive as we struggle with problems of our own. Would this young boy have grown up and rebelled against Christ, forfeiting his place in paradise? We cannot be sure. But implicit to the possibility is the unwavering assurance that God is good, He is trustworthy, and it is best to follow Him, whether you understand Him or not. That is how I want to live, and I hope you will too.

DISCUSSION QUESTIONS

1. Has the suffering of others ever caused fear in your own heart?
2. What is the thin line between questioning God and correcting Him?
3. Why do you suppose both faith and fear manifest during the same hardship?
4. What does God's response to Job teach you about your greatest need?

ELEVEN LIGHT AT THE END OF THE TUNNEL

Have you ever watched Spider-Man get his blood pressure checked? The sight of Carson dressed as the Marvel comic hero not only left me grinning but also brought laughter to the nurses who welcomed us. Our friends at the Pensacola airport had purchased the costume as a gift and had given it to Carson before we boarded our flight. The disguise was perfect because it covered his face, making his medical mask unnecessary. He not only loved it but also refused to take it off. We walked through the terminal shooting webs at imaginary villains.

When we arrived in Memphis, Carson insisted on wearing his super suit to the hospital for his evening blood work. All the nurses played along, and some even thanked him for saving the day. Even after returning to our room for the night, I had to peel the costume off him in order to tuck my superhero into bed. The iconic images of that day still bring a smile to my face. The incident is just one example, though it may sound strange, of all the fun we had on our trips to St. Jude.

Because of moments like these, the long days turned into weeks, and the weeks became years. It initially seemed like we would never hit the finish line, but soon we were just weeks

Fun at St. Jude—Carson was
Spider-Man the entire trip!

away from Carson's final chemo treatment. After so many ups and downs, the light at the end of the tunnel was not just visible; it was beautifully bright. Things could not have been better for us. Carson's hair was back. His body was responding better to the cocktail of medication he received each week. Our routine was set. Finally, it seemed like we were winning the long battle that had consumed every part of our lives the previous few years. The end, along with the outcome we prayed for, was in sight.

As I look back over all the small joys we shared along the way, I am eternally grateful for each one. What father has the privilege of spending thirty-six straight hours with his son every week? Because our third son, Jacob, was born during our first year of traveling to St. Jude, my wife was unable to alternate trips to Memphis like we originally planned. That meant Carson and I shared precious time I wouldn't trade for the world. I realize now that these small gifts from the Lord along the way were part of a bigger picture. Reading about it in the Bible is not the same as living it each day. What am I referring to? In a word—*peace*.

People often ask me how we endured such a lengthy trial. It was not until I learned the unrestricted impact of God's peace on my life that I was able to be still while the Lord worked. To prepare us for our most tenuous moments, the apostle Paul commands, "Be anxious for nothing, but in everything by prayer and supplication with thanksgiving let your requests be made known to God. And the peace of God, which surpasses all comprehension, will guard your hearts and your minds in Christ Jesus" (Philippians 4:6–7).

In one sense, God's powerful, abundant peace defies explanation. My inability to elucidate the rich nuances of this heavenly endowment does not diminish its importance, however. Perhaps a brief description of how God's peace impacted our lives will be more helpful than a cold definition anyway. It was the Lord's peace that prevented us from dwelling on an unknown future. Peace that calmed us when unexpected obstacles arose. Peace that taught us to be patient when we wanted to hurry. Peace that helped us rest when everything around us was tumultuous. Peace that persuaded us to remain silent when we wanted to speak. Peace that emboldened us to entrust our son to the Savior we follow. Apart from God's peace, I cannot imagine facing any of life's calamities. The same peace is available to you.

REFOCUSED PRIORITIES

One of the daunting impairments of any adversity is the worry that accompanies it. Speculating over outcomes while processing your best course of action is both overwhelming and anxiety laden. One benefit, however, is the forced reexamination of what is truly significant in our lives. Nothing whittles away our frivolous ambitions like the incessant reminder that most of our obsessions do not really matter. Stated differently, most of what we worry about is not that important and should be abandoned.

Throughout Carson's ordeal, three guiding priorities rose to greatest prominence in my life. First, how can we glorify God throughout the duration of this fight? Second, what must I do to make certain that my son will be well again? Third, how can I protect my family in the meantime?

Though other issues deserved attention, I realized only these would receive *my attention*. The size of my financial portfolio was of no concern. Climbing the denominational ladder of success in ministry was now irrelevant. What others thought of me did not occupy any of my energies. Suffering removed the trivialities from our lives because there was simply no room for them. In this sense, your burden may be one of God's greatest gifts to you.

While writing from a Roman prison cell, the apostle Paul's prized aspirations emerged. Instead of imposing upon the Philippian church, he pleads for their spiritual growth and maturity: "Only conduct yourselves in a manner worthy of the gospel of Christ" was his earnest appeal (Philippians 1:27). Living in a way that is worthy of the gospel, in other words, is what life is all about. Paul then added:

> Make my joy complete by being of the same mind, maintaining the same love, united in spirit, intent on one purpose. Do nothing from selfishness or empty conceit, but with humility of mind regard one another as more important than yourselves; do not merely look out for your own personal interests, but also for the interests of others.
>
> *Philippians 2:2–4*

The sheer joy of basic devotion to the Lord was the driving factor behind these words. The commands, though simple, are laser focused. Do not be selfish, conceited, or proud. Stop looking out for yourself to the detriment of others. The goal is not to be in charge, look important, throw your weight around, or win every argument. Life is too short and eternity is too long for our conduct to reflect petty matters.

Still not ready to shed the frivolous in your life? Consider how the humility of Jesus reflected His eternal priorities:

> Have this attitude in yourselves which was also in Christ Jesus, who, although He existed in the form of God, did not regard equality with God a thing to be grasped, but emptied Himself, taking the form of a bond-servant, and being made in the likeness of men. Being found in appearance as a man, He humbled Himself by becoming obedient to the point of death, even death on a cross.
>
> *Philippians 2:5–8*

Refusing to live for Himself, Jesus utilized every occasion as an opportunity to sacrifice for others. His were no small matters either. The king became a servant. The infinite became finite. The divine became human. The light of the world endured the darkness of the cross. No ambitions for fame, wealth, or power. Rather than glorify Himself, He submitted to His Father. The most excruciating hardships in Jesus' life *reinforced* these commitments rather than *competed with* them. Our Savior continually *reaffirmed* His priorities rather than *dismissed* them. Likewise, our deepest wounds will necessarily push our greatest resolutions to the forefront. Using the example of Jesus to motivate us, Paul returned to the theme of intentional living:

Do all things without grumbling or disputing; so that you will prove yourselves to be blameless and innocent, children of God above reproach in the midst of a crooked and perverse generation, among whom you appear as lights in the world, holding fast the word of life, so that in the day of Christ I will have reason to glory because I did not run in vain nor toil in vain.

Philippians 2:14–16

In every circumstance and challenge, God wants us to grow in the Spirit, obey His Word, share His gospel, and honor His name. Far too much of our anxiousness derives from factors outside of these essentials. Without the interruption of heartache, we can easily become so self-absorbed that we forget our mission to become like Christ and reach others for Him. Trials are a wonderful opportunity to reset our most significant priorities.

THE KEY TO OVERCOMING WORRY

Worry shows up in a variety of places. We worry about our work, our kids, our health, our bills, our marriage, and our future. You will find it between the steps paced nervously on a floor. Or behind the wrinkles on a forehead lost in a sea of possibilities. It might show up in a deafening silence that drowns out the day's laughter. But wherever and whenever you find it, worry robs us of the peace God wants us to know. When worry increases, faith decreases. So many of my worst fears during Carson's illness never came to fruition, yet they caused numerous sleepless nights nonetheless.

Jesus repeatedly admonished His followers to resist worry as a sinful deviation from trusting our heavenly Father. In fact, He taught that continually fretting over what we cannot control is more descriptive of an unbeliever than a Christ-follower. To prove His point, our Savior pointed to the birds of the air, who do not reap or sow and yet never lack food due to God's sustained provision for them (Matthew 6:26). Likewise, the lilies of the field clothe the hillside with greater beauty than any article in Solomon's wardrobe when, outside of our Lord's efforts, they would not be there (6:28–30). The implication is one of priority; our responsibility is to seek God's kingdom above all else while trusting the Lord to take care of us in all other matters (6:33). A failure to do so is an affront, not only to the providential care our God provides, but also to the goodness that characterizes Him. "Do not worry about tomorrow," Jesus said, "for tomorrow will care for itself. Each day has enough trouble of its own" (6:34).

When worry increases, faith decreases.

What, then, is the key to overcoming the situations that cause us panic? Let's return to Paul's previous statement about the peace of God (Philippians 4:6–7). The greatest defense against the anxieties that wreak havoc in our lives is consistent, focused *prayer* and *supplication*. The former is the Bible's general word for addressing the Father, while the latter captures those desperate times when we express our particular needs to Him. We offer any and all petitions to the Lord *with thanksgiving* even before the Lord answers us. Doing so reveals our submission to God's plan and our confidence in His will. We are free to bring any request before the Lord after we resign ourselves to praise Him, no matter the outcome.

Do we trust Him enough to express our gratitude regardless of what His answer might be? If so, Scripture assures us that God's peace will guard our *hearts* and *minds* in Christ Jesus (Philippians 4:7). Years ago, a friend of mine shared an exercise with me that captures the principle of peace through prayer beautifully. He suggested that from time to time I make two lists on the same sheet of paper, separated only by a line down the middle of the page. I title the left side *My Worry List*. I label the right side *My Prayer List*. Then when apprehension or trepidation rears its ugly head, I list each of my concerns in the left column. As I pray about each item, however, I cross it out and move it to my prayer list. Remarkably, when my prayer list is full, my worry list is empty!

Perhaps the sheer fact that you picked up this book indicates that something or someone is causing you much sorrow. I assure you, *God can handle it*. The apostle Peter admonishes, "Humble yourselves under the mighty hand of God, that He may exalt you at the proper time, casting all your anxiety on Him, because He cares for you" (1 Peter 5:6–7). Pour out your heart to God in prayer, knowing His concern, and redirect your focus to His blessings in your life.

LIFTING YOUR GAZE

Once we release our troubles to the Lord through agonizing petition, it is crucial that we lift our emotional gaze so as to avoid the heavy yokes of agitation and disruption that so often accompany our afflictions. What you choose to dwell on will, in large part, determine whether or not you eschew the heaviness of worry. Thus we read, "Finally, brethren, whatever is true, whatever is honorable, whatever is right, whatever is pure, whatever is lovely, whatever is of good repute, if there is any excellence and if anything worthy of praise, dwell on these things" (Philippians 4:8).

By meditating on what is true, honorable, right, pure, lovely, and good, our minds remain secure within the comfort Christ affords us. Let me show you how God eases our despair through what we give our attention to.

Whatever is true. So many of our earthly frustrations stem from a selfish worldview that contradicts God's Word. Lured away by the deceitfulness of riches, we live for the material instead of the eternal (I Timothy 6:9–10). Enticed by the possibility of a trouble-free life, we measure God's faithfulness by our circumstances rather than vice versa (John 16:33). Hungry for relationships that exist for our personal fulfillment, we resent the needs of others as inconsiderate intrusions while ignoring commandments to the contrary (Romans 12:3, 10–13). Each of these misplaced aspirations creates significant grief that could be avoided simply by ordering our lives according to the teachings of Scripture. Saturating our minds with God's truth enables us to release much of the needless anguish we carry.

Prioritizing truth forced our family to ignore the emotions and doubts that continually competed for our allegiance. We refused to denounce God's goodness. We tried not to question God's right to do whatever He wished in our lives. We rejected the old deception that God was angry with us. We reminded ourselves that our Lord loves Carson even more than we do. We rested in the Master's blueprint for our lives, even when it was mysterious. Again and again, we insisted to ourselves that we exist for God's glory. Shining the light of God's truth on the lies in our hearts kept us sane throughout the entirety of these turbulent years.

Whatever is honorable. When we abandon worldly pursuits, it is much easier to celebrate things worthy of respect. In relation to our trials, this could mean dwelling on their sanctifying impact instead of on other outcomes we prefer. Considering God's work *in us* enabled us to survive the chaos that was *around us*. Though I never felt like the Lord was chastening us for a specific shortcoming in our faith, I am certain He worked aggressively to transform us into the image of Christ. Simply choosing to fix our hearts on God's honorable end instead of on His chosen means relieved our misery.

Whatever is right. With an emphasis on God's justice, this phrase compels us to value true fairness more than our immediate relief. The directive also requires that we trust God for vengeance when others do us wrong. Is your confidence in God strong enough for you to resist moral shortcuts despite their expedience? Will you let Him settle the score when someone hurts you? Despite the few who actively sought to discourage us during Carson's leukemia battle, we decided to draw strength from the hundreds of supporters who undergirded us. Refusing to worry about people and factors we could not control, we sought to glorify God and take care of our son. Remember, it is never wrong to do what is right.

Whatever is pure. Being in the world while remaining unlike the world is easier said than done. Celebrating what God values will anchor us to a heavenly perspective, regardless of our unpleasant experiences. Thus, holiness should be more important to us than easy living. The purity and authenticity of laying our struggles before the Lord can be a source of great satisfaction if we let it. Without our realizing it, vain and frivolous ambitions can creep into our lives. Watching God purge our lives of these nefarious temptations became a joyful exercise in the end.

Whatever is lovely. Recognizing the fingerprints of the Lord and the beauty of all that He has made is a healthy distraction when times are tough. When we allow self-pity to demoralize us, we miss the wonder of small treasures and moments that happen every day. Instead, God wants us to enjoy His gifts in creation, His handiwork in others, and His grace in the simple pleasures of life.

Time will not permit me to list each of the lovely gifts we received from the Lord during our nearly three-year stint with cancer. Seeing my son Brady take his first steps down the long hallway at the Ronald McDonald House was a needed pick-me-up on an otherwise difficult day. Welcoming my third son, Jacob, at the end of Carson's first year of chemotherapy was a healthy distraction for the remainder of his treatment. Meeting a stranger in the airport who led his company to send our family to Rupp Arena for a Kentucky Wildcats basketball game transformed another mundane trip into something spectacular. Cheering as Carson threw out the first pitch at a Pensacola Blue Wahoos baseball game further endeared us to the Delta team who arranged it. Welcoming the "real" Spider-Man to Carson's fifth birthday party (also made possible by our airport friends) is something our family still talks about. On and on I could go, but I am simply illustrating that God's blessings usually exceed our troubles, if only we resolve to notice.

Whatever is of good repute. What we hear and what we say to others can dramatically enhance or limit our ability to rest in God's watch care over our lives. Rather than mulling over every painful incident and verbalizing its reality and harshness, we should think and speak carefully, focusing on life's blessings instead. Thus, we chose to dream about Carson's future instead of bemoaning the misfortune of his present. *How will God use him? How will he be able to help others? How will God be glorified through our son?* These were all normal questions that wove the fabric of perseverance into our lives.

By lifting your gaze to these noble emphases, you will find it much easier to leave your distress with the Lord after you lay it down. Throughout Carson's sickness, there were so many moments we almost missed because of our preoccupation with his needs. Thankfully, God helped us realize through prayer that, even while fighting cancer, ours was a story of manifold blessings worth dwelling on.

DISCUSSION QUESTIONS

1. To what degree would you say you have experienced God's peace?
2. How do worldly distractions restrict your ability to rest in God's peace?
3. What priorities should drive your life if you want to resist anxiety?

TWELVE

WHEN THE DAWN BREAKS

My eyes welled up with tears. As I surveyed the room, I could not believe the day had finally come. Sitting in one of three purple leather chairs that adorned the medicine room, Carson removed his shirt so that Nurse Emily could access his port. It had already been a long day. Earlier, a brain MRI and a bone marrow draw made it necessary to sedate Carson, leaving him a bit groggy. Still, this was the moment we had anticipated for nearly three years.

In a plastic bag beside the chair was a clear vial filled with the yellow drug methotrexate. Our favorite nurses gathered round, along with members of our family who had made the trip to Memphis, to witness what would be Carson's final dose of chemotherapy. After months of praying and fighting as hard as we could, the long journey was about to end. With the slow push of a thumb, the last drop of medicine needed to cure his leukemia entered his body. After deaccessing the plastic tube attached to his chest, the nurses broke out into song:

Our patients have the cutest S-M-I-L-Es;
 our patients have the sweetest H-E-A-R-Ts.

Oh we love to see you every day,
but now is the time we get to say,
Pack up your bags, get out the door,
you don't get chemo anymore!

It was finally over.

The magnitude of this milestone was not lost on us even before we arrived in Memphis. The Delta Airlines team at our local airport planned a special surprise for their favorite passenger's last flight to St. Jude. We were seated in our usual 10B and 10C when the captain announced over the loudspeaker, "Ladies and gentlemen. We have a special guest on this morning's flight. After more than a hundred trips to St. Jude Hospital in Memphis for chemotherapy, Carson Dooley is making his final journey today. As we taxi to the runway, please turn your attention outside as we celebrate with a full water salute."

The ceremonial water salute typically marks the retirement of a senior pilot or the last flight of an aircraft after a long career. Today, however, the local fire department showed up to celebrate my son's accomplishment. With fire trucks positioned on both sides of our plane, plumes of water formed an arch over us as we passed under. Carson was beaming. My wife and I took pictures of the scene. And the passengers on our plane cheered wildly. The applause put a lump in my throat as I tried to hold it together.

Now six years old, my son still had a baby face, but an intrusive maturity now peered through his young eyes. In noticing how much he had grown, I realized he would continue growing and, even more important, *living*. Our nightmare was coming to an end, and Carson was emerging victorious. Finally the dawn was breaking, and, as promised, I wanted to shout for joy (Psalm 30:5).

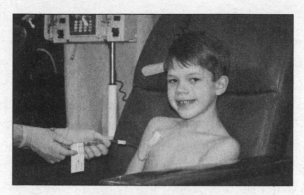

Last day of chemo!

Even more remarkable to me was the recognition that none of the celebration and satisfaction filling my heart would have been possible apart from the depth of the valley we were coming out of and the darkness of the night that was finally breaking around us. For the first time, not only was I grateful for Carson's healing, but I also felt a strange appreciation that God had allowed us to walk through this trial. The same burden that led me to question God previously was now wooing me to worship Him like never before. Do not misunderstand. I hate cancer, and I would never choose such a difficult path for my son. Yet I recognize the profound impact this ordeal had on my family, especially Carson. The lessons we learned are like pearls of wisdom that money cannot buy. I realize, like never before, how ill-equipped I am to determine the best path for my loved ones or myself.

THE ATTITUDE CHECK WE NEED

Job seemed to learn similar lessons. The end of his saga reads more like an apology letter than the heroic conclusion we expect. After hearing directly from the Lord (Job 38–41), the tested servant confesses God's absolute sovereignty over his life (42:2). Though he did not repent of any hidden transgression, as suggested by his friends, Job realized that his tone and attitude toward his heavenly Father had become disrespectful. He had spoken what he did not know. He had judged unfairly what he did not understand. And worse still, he had harbored bitterness toward the Lord, casting Him as an enemy to overcome (42:3). Recognizing the audacity of his claims, Job repented for his harsh rhetoric and sinful attitude (42:4–6).

Remember, this was a man whom God considered to be more righteous than any living person on the earth (Job 1:8; 2:3). Yet he, like us, needed time to mature and grow. Surrendering to God's complete ownership over our lives was not easy then, nor is it easy today. Yet Job enables us to see the beauty and peace of total surrender to the Lord. His life reminds us that our frustrations and bewilderments do not grant us permission to challenge or correct our God. Asking God why is always permissible, but we are in no position to demand His answer (see chapter 1). Questioning the Creator is allowed; chastising Him for what He allows is out of bounds. Telling the Lord how you feel is welcomed; rebelling because of those feelings is not.

Herein lies the attitude adjustment we all need. Our confusion over *how God works* should never diminish our confidence in *who God is*. Surrendering to Him does *not* mean that we enjoy the pain that invades our lives, but that we choose to trust Him anyway. Our temporary setbacks and agonies do not force the eternal God of heaven and earth to explain Himself. We are foolish to think otherwise. He *is* God, and we are *not*! Job embodies the desirable humility of Romans 11:33–36:

Oh, the depth of the riches both of the wisdom and knowledge of God! How unsearchable are His judgments and unfathomable His ways! For who has known the mind of the Lord, or who became His counselor? Or who has first given to Him that it might be paid back to him again? For from Him and through Him and to Him are all things. To Him be the glory forever. Amen.

You likely picked up this book because either you or someone you love is hurting. Perhaps vivid, agonizing distress litters the scenes of what should have been joyous occasions in your life. Are you bitter toward God because of your past? Are anger and resentment over what you do not understand destroying your relationship with Christ? Are you distant from or even rebellious toward God because, in your mind, He cannot be trusted? May I offer a loving word of biblical correction? The solution is *your repentance*, not *God's explanation*. Deep wounds leave us vulnerable to inverting our appreciation for the Sovereign of the universe because of a preoccupation with ourselves.

Our confusion over *how God works* should never diminish our confidence in *who God is*.

Though I do not doubt the substantial trauma in your life, we must be careful not to exalt ourselves above the Lord by believing the deceptive lie that our comfort should be His primary agenda.

Just one glimpse of the Lord drives us to repentance. Truly, Job suffered greatly. And no, he did not deserve the trials he faced. Yet God had reasons for it that, as far as we know, Job never understood. The same may be true of you. The commotion pillaging your life may be for no fault of your own. Resist the assumption that you know better than God what you need or the urge to take matters into your own hands. Job realized his error and forsook it. We are wise to do the same.

WHEN THE DUST SETTLES

After Job forgave his friends for their callous accusations, the Lord fully restored him (Job 42:10–17). With his fortunes returned, his relationships healed, and his heart full, Job learned that there is life after trials. Even more importantly, he learned that God was faithful, no matter what he faced. Our experience was similar. After his last dose of chemotherapy, Carson returned to St. Jude a month later to have his subcutaneous port surgically removed. Again, we cried, celebrated, and stood in awe of God's goodness toward us. He really is faithful.

An unexpected dilemma, however, lurked beneath the surface of God's blessings in our lives. Even as we glorified the Lord for His protection of Carson, I initially felt guilty for enjoying the victory that so many others could not. Many families leave St. Jude without their babies. Not every adversity evaporates after long seasons of prayer and waiting. At first glance, it often appears that far too many of life's burdens will never go away.

Maybe that is your story. For you, God did not heal. Perhaps you are still making trips to a hospital for treatments of some kind. Though the verdict is not entirely in, you know what's ahead after your doctor labeled your condition *terminal*. You may have had to stand over the casket of a loved one, even though you begged God for a miracle. Or maybe your adversity is not life-threatening, but it seems just as severe. Your marriage fell apart despite your pleas for forgiveness. Though you promised to work harder, you still lost your job. Repeated appeals and messages notwithstanding, your friend will not call back. After years of therapy, your addiction still haunts you nonetheless. Despite your best efforts to forget the past, the abusive sins of someone you trusted, or even a complete stranger, weigh you down like a ball and chain. While everyone around you seems to be thriving, you just cannot catch a break.

Instead of celebrating the long-awaited answer to prayer, you're dealing with trouble that seems to have no solution. Broken relationships remain. Gloomy prognoses discourage. Enslaving habits injure. Relentless pain tortures. Whatever it might be, you spend your time . . .

Waiting.

Wondering.

Grieving.

Hurting.

Coping with oppressive realities like these will test even the most mature faith. Though God does not always change our circumstances, *He is still faithful.* We should never measure the goodness of our Lord by the difficulty of the immediate. With eternity as our backdrop, we rest, knowing that God will ultimately restore all that this fallen world steals from us. Writing about the relief we long for, the apostle John predicted, "[God] will wipe away every tear from their eyes; and there will no longer be any death; there will no longer be any mourning, or crying, or pain; the first things have passed away" (Revelation 21:4). With the curse of Eden lifted, we will be free to enjoy the blessings of God's creation forever. The most excruciating hardships we face now will seem like temporary intrusions in the life to come.

Though it is impossible for us to fathom God's methods, plans, or timing, we can trust that He loves us. He is a Warrior who defends us, a Shepherd who leads us, and a Strong Tower we should run *to* rather than *from*. He is *not* to be blamed for our afflictions. God proves His faithfulness to us in two ways. Sometimes He removes our troubles and relieves our pain; other times He sustains us until the light of eternity illuminates both the purpose *behind* and the reward *for* our deepest struggles. In both cases, the Lord is a rock on which the foundation of our life remains strong.

In the years that immediately followed Carson's completion of chemotherapy, I struggled with knowing that our son lived while other young patients did not. I have come to realize, however, that God is not less faithful to our friends at St. Jude who lost their children than He is to us. To the contrary, the Lord often proves His faithfulness, not by taking our problems away, but by walking with us until He does. Whether He relieves us now, as in our case, or in heaven, as with so many others, our Savior promises to take care of His own. When we meet Him face-to-face, no one will question His goodness. In the meantime, our task is to trust Him, regardless of the outcomes we may encounter. In other words, the issue is not how our storms end, but whether or not our feet remain firmly planted on the rock that is Jesus Christ (Matthew 7:24–27).

Whether He relieves us now or in heaven, our Savior promises to take care of His own.

ALL GLORY TO GOD

I am still amazed by the breadth of Carson's long battle. All told, my little warrior experienced . . .

- 20 lumbar punctures
- 9 different types of chemotherapy
- 8 hospitalizations due to fever
- 3 bone marrow draws
- more flights than I could count
- even more hours in the car

For 134 weeks, he fought for his life every day. Today he is healthy and thriving. I cannot thank the Lord enough for Carson's remarkable recovery. If you saw him now, you would never know he once had childhood cancer. Just as King David praised God for his deliverance, my heart also rejoices: "I will give thanks to You, O LORD, among the nations, and I will sing praises to Your name" (2 Samuel 22:50).

We marked Carson's last day at St. Jude with a "No Mo Chemo" cake. Later we celebrated with a trip to Disney World, thanks to the generosity of the Make-A-Wish Foundation. Our family even relocated in order to have a completely new start. More recently, we began organizing "Carson and Friends" events to raise money for our favorite hospital and to raise awareness about childhood cancer. Thankfully, I have been able to share in churches all over the Southeast how God saved my son's life. I look forward to the day when Carson will be old enough to speak for himself. But more than anything, our hearts overflow with joy and gratitude for God's continued grace and mercy in our lives.

No matter your challenges or triumphs, my prayer is that you, too, will worship the Lord with no strings attached. As an open vessel before the King of the universe, trust Him, follow Him, rest in Him, rely on Him, and, above all, exalt Him. Bless the Lord and His holy name with all your soul—with all that is within you (Psalm 103:1).

DISCUSSION QUESTIONS

1. How does the end of a trial change your perception of God's work in our lives?

2. How does your desire for comfort often distort your view of God?

3. What valuable lessons has the suffering in your life taught you?

4. How should you respond to God when your circumstances do not resolve like you hoped they would?

5. Why is it so difficult to worship God when troubles are present?

THIRTEEN

LIFE WILL NEVER
BE THE SAME

Though I knew this day would come, it was far more difficult than I ever imagined. I tried not to stare, but my eyes locked in amazement on the confident, handsome boy before me. His hair was thick and shiny. His cheeks were slim, free from any steroids. No port protruded from beneath his shirt. None of his bones ached due to medication. His smile was uninterrupted by the fear in his eyes. He looked wonderfully normal. After Carson made it through six months of being cancer-free, no visible signs betrayed all that this little warrior had gone through. This was his first day of school.

Because of our trips to St. Jude and his need for a germ-free environment, Heather homeschooled Carson for kindergarten. After three years of dreaming about his being able to live an ordinary life without the heavy concerns that childhood cancer brings, we saw that day finally arrive, marked by the beginning of his first-grade year. Everything was new for us. After relocating to Texas, I was pastoring a new congregation. We were living in a new home in a new place and were making new friends. Carson had a new school and a new life to begin.

I held my tears back, but the lump in my throat made it

Carson's first day of school

difficult to speak. The protective bubble we created for Carson's survival was no longer necessary. My apprehension was tangible, however. *How will the other students treat him? Is his immune system ready to fight off the typical viruses kids pick up at school? Will he have any side effects that will make it difficult for him to learn? Is he ready to be away from us after being so dependent on Heather and me these last three years? Who will run interference for him? Will anyone notice if he needs anything? Is he scared?* On and on it went as my mind raced with uncomfortable scenarios of Carson being vulnerable.

Sensing that Heather was feeling the same, I took her by the hand. Without saying a word, we both knew and understood how equally exciting and terrifying this moment was. With my best friend beside me and my precious son before me, it felt like we were stepping off the battlefield victorious but wounded. Though we had put down our weapons, the smoke of war still hovered over our souls. God gave us what we prayed for, and now it was time to loosen our grip and enjoy the spoils of our new life together.

Carson seemed a bit nervous, but no different from what any child experiences on the first day of school. His mother and I dropped to one knee, hugged him tightly, and said, "Do you know how proud we are of you?"

"Yes," he answered, "and you know I am going to be fine, right?" Like so many other times throughout his journey, Carson was there for us just like we were always there for him.

"No doubt in my mind, son!" I said with a smile. "I love you so much."

"I love you too, Dad."

I kissed him on the forehead, watched him take his seat, and then stared a bit longer, hoping he wouldn't see me. As Heather and I walked back down the hallway to leave, I put one arm around her as I turned my head the opposite direction, hoping she would not see me wipe a tear from my cheek with my other hand. Getting on with our lives was more challenging than I anticipated, but it was time to begin.

THE BATTLE YOU CANNOT WIN

The strange incident of Jacob wrestling with God has always fascinated me, probably because its meaning is not immediately obvious. Dramatic overtones set the stage for the patriarch's divine encounter and transformation. With a name that bears the idea of being a *deceiver*, Isaac's younger son lived up to his reputation repeatedly. As his estranged brother approaches, Jacob turns to his old tricks in order to protect himself. Fearing Esau's anger over his lost birthright (Genesis 25:19–34), Jacob pretends to be his servant (32:3–4). In addition to this manipulative sleight of hand, Jacob also attempts to bribe his brother by offering him numerous animals as a gift, not once but twice (32:5, 13–20). Even when it seems like these deceptive shenanigans have failed, he attempts to dupe the Lord in prayer by misquoting

His promises (see 32:9–12, in light of Genesis 28:14–15). Jacob had nowhere to turn but to God; yet he still found it difficult to trust Him.

After sending his family away for their own protection (Genesis 32:22–23), Jacob was finally alone and vulnerable. He thought Esau was his greatest threat, but God was the real predator. After years of struggle and resistance, the Lord was ready to break Jacob. The text simply says that "a man wrestled with him until daybreak" (32:24). Though Jacob was initially unaware of his opponent's identity, the patriarch's challenger was God Himself. Determined to eradicate his pride and stubbornness, the Hound of Heaven pounced on his unsuspecting target. Like so many of us, the Old Testament *deceiver* would have to be bruised before he was useful to his Master. I see so much of myself in these verses.

Just months before Carson's illness, I had the privilege of hiring a new staff member, who became a tremendous asset to our team in Alabama. During the interview, he answered patiently as I asked him numerous questions about his life, theology, and ministry. After responding to each of my inquiries, I gave him the opportunity to ask me anything he wanted. "Just one thing," he said. "What is the worst trial you ever walked through?" I thought for a moment, and then, somewhat embarrassed, I admitted that my life had been fairly easy. "Nothing comes to mind," I said. "Aside from a few minor incidents, most of my life has been trouble-free." I will never forget his reply. "Oh no!" he exclaimed. "We are going to face some major challenges together."

He was right. But why are difficulties so instrumental in our spiritual development? Because God reserves His greatest blessings for the weakest recipients. The Lord unapologetically chooses to use not the powerful but the weak. From heaven's perspective, the foolish shame the wise, and the weak reduce the strong to nothing (1 Corinthians 1:26–29). Because God perfects His strength through weakness, His power rests on the battered instead of the whole (2 Corinthians 12:9). Trials, like nothing else, pivot our focus away from our superficial importance back to the One who refuses to share His glory with anyone (Isaiah 42:8). Stated simply, God must break us before He can use us.

The night that Jacob spent fighting against God to retain control of his life was a parable of his entire existence. Observing that his will remained untamed, the Lord touched Jacob's hip, inflicting him with a lifelong injury (Genesis 32:25). After

> **Because God perfects His strength through weakness, His power rests on the battered instead of the whole.**

years of cunning schemes against his brother, father, and father-in-law, the patriarch recognized he was finally outmatched. Forecasting his impending defeat, Jacob pled for a blessing from his adversary (32:26). With a response much like waving a white flag, the stubborn manipulator finally humbled himself in order to receive God's mercy. The craftiness in his past melted away as Jacob became desperate for divine power in his life.

Remarkably, the Lord graciously took Jacob back to his first exercise in self-importance. The question "What is your name?" is less a reflection of God's ignorance and more His effort to break Jacob's ego for good (Genesis 32:27). By identifying himself, the patriarch essentially admitted he was a deceiver. In addition, the inquiry takes us back to the first time someone asked Jacob his name. In that case, it was his father Isaac who said, "Who are you, my son?" (27:18). On that occasion, Jacob not only lied but also appeared to do so successfully. Now, out of options, he saw himself as the Lord did and admitted his true character (32:27). And what did God do in return? He gave him a new name! Jacob became Israel ("God fights for you"), not due to his exploitive schemes, but because of God's amazing grace (32:28).

Thus the Lord declared, "You have striven with God and with men and have prevailed." And how did Jacob prevail? Not by his strength or wisdom, but by means of his surrender. God is affirming that Jacob won by losing. He did not overpower the Lord, but instead he reached a point of victory because he learned to yield. Our heavenly Father does the same for us. When we learn that the way up is down, we inherit new names, as the Lord declares us to be righteous through faith (Romans 5:1):

- **Liar** used to describe you. Now you are a **Child of Truth**.
- **Hypocrite** was your name. Now you are a **New Creation**.
- Before you were **Enslaved**. Now you are **Free**.
- A former **Sinner**. Now a **Saint**.

Broken triumph is not only the doorway into God's family; it is also the pathway to becoming useful in His kingdom.

WALKING WITH A LIMP

As the sun rose after Jacob's encounter with the Lord, he continued on his journey, but only with a limp (Genesis 32:31). In fact, the Old Testament reveals, "To this day the sons of Israel do not eat the sinew of the hip which is on the socket of the thigh, because he touched the socket of Jacob's thigh in the sinew of the hip" (32:32). In other words, after God breaks you, life is never the same.

Things certainly have not been the same for us since Carson's recovery. Though he is thriving as a young boy, I still smell the smoke from our battlefield occasionally. Sometimes it is a nightmare about our most painful moments that wakes me in a cold sweat. Other times it is an unexpected tear due to a St. Jude commercial on television. The news of another child's diagnosis usually evokes forgotten fears that were our routine previously. For reasons I cannot explain, I often stare at Carson while wrestling down fears of a possible relapse in the future. I frequently rub his hair while saying a silent prayer for him. Some days I feel melancholy with no apparent explanation. Being overprotective is a constant struggle. Life has gone on for us, thankfully, but we are limping nonetheless.

These scars are blessings in disguise, however. So many sanctifying by-products emerged from our hardship too. Little annoyances do not bother me quite like they once did. My personal ambitions are much less about me now and much more about God's glory. After testing so much of what I teach others, I believe more than ever that God's Word is true and reliable. What God knows about me takes precedence over what people think about me now. My wife and I share a love and admiration for each other that only comes after walking together through a deep valley. She was, and is, the glue that holds our family together. Celebrating each moment with all of our children (now five total!) is a much greater priority to me today than it was before.

Once you learn to depend fully on God, resting in your own strength and wisdom is never enough again. These lessons have not come easy for us. I still wrestle with my pride. I still battle my ego. Sadly, I still want to demand my own way at times. Yet the anchors that pull me back to surrender are much stronger now. After tasting the peace that comes with yielding to your heavenly Father, reassuming control of your life is much less enticing. Learning to limp is one of the best things that ever happened to me. Life will never be the same, but truthfully, I don't want it to be.

DISCUSSION QUESTIONS

1. Have you found it difficult to move on after a traumatic experience?
2. Why does God choose to use the weak rather than the strong?
3. In what areas of your life do you need to surrender more fully to the Lord?

EPILOGUE

Writing this book was more difficult than I expected. Reliving these moments brought back waves of emotion that I did not anticipate. Today Carson is completely healthy, excelling in his schoolwork and sports. A few years ago, I had the privilege of baptizing him after his profession of faith in Christ. We rejoice and give God thanks that we are in a very different place now than we were before. Looking back is painful, but it remains instructive for us. Our family is better after walking through this valley. Though the scars of these recollections remain, so do the life-changing lessons and the fuller intimacy with the Lord they produced.

My prayer is that these experiences and all that God taught us through them will be a helpful guide when you navigate life's darkest moments. Toward that end, I would be remiss if I did not alert you to the foundational commitment that precedes every assurance and blessing I have outlined in these pages: *God reserves His promises for His people.* Before you dare to believe that God is always with you, that He is purposeful in your suffering, and that He is actively working everything in your life for good, you *must* have a personal relationship with Jesus Christ. The Bible simply says you must be born again (John 3:3).

And how can a person be born again? Outside of the person

and work of Jesus Christ, the salvation we desperately need is impossible. The story of Jesus' death on the cross and His resurrection from the dead is not a fairy tale meant to entertain us, nor is it merely a good example intended to inspire us. God Himself stepped into human history, took on human flesh, lived among us, and died as a sacrifice for each of us (John 3:16). But why was this necessary?

Since the Garden of Eden, sin interrupted our relationship with God and guaranteed our death. Because all people are born sinners, the devastating consequences of our transgression are everywhere. Much of this book chronicles the ever-present burdens we live with because our world is fallen. Though not every trial is the direct result of our personal disobedience, each of us is a sinner in need of a Savior (Romans 3:23). Because God is holy, we too must be holy in order to be in His family.

Thus, God chose to intervene through His Son, Jesus Christ. By living a sinless life, Jesus became a suitable sacrifice for our sins (Mark 15). Not only does His death take away our wickedness, but His resurrection also imparts His righteous perfection to all who will believe in His name (2 Corinthians 5:21). These are historical facts that can change your life! Christ died for your sins; He was buried; and He rose from the dead three days later (1 Corinthians 15:3–4). Consequently, He offers salvation to us, or the forgiveness of our sins, as a free gift of His grace (Ephesians 2:8–9).

The most important question, then, is how can we receive this wonderful gift God has provided? Simply put, through repentance and faith. "Unless you repent," Jesus warned, "you will all likewise perish" (Luke 13:3, 5). Realizing that sin severed our relationship with the Lord, we must humbly ask God to forgive us and strive to forsake our old way of life. As we turn away from the person we used to be, we need to embrace Jesus Christ in faith as our Lord and Savior. Believing that He died for us and rose from the grave, we submit our lives to Christ as the King of kings and Lord of lords (Romans 10:9–10). If you will call out to Christ, seeking His grace, He *will save you* (10:13). This is what it means to be born again.

I cannot imagine enduring the hardships of life without leaning on the promises of Scripture and resting in the presence of my Savior. He sustained us during Carson's illness. He is good! He is strong! He is trustworthy! And He is always there! May you find the same joy, no matter what trials invade your life. God loves you. He is not your enemy. Trust Him. Run to Him and find comfort.

Today our family is healthy, thriving, and growing!

DISCUSSION QUESTIONS

1. What biblical promises in this book are the most meaningful to you?
2. How can you be sure that you are born again?

ACKNOWLEDGMENTS

Every book is a labor of love, but this project has been particularly gratifying because of all the people who journeyed with us through the experience. For those of you who walked beside us, prayed for us, encouraged us—thank you. The body of Christ is more real to me than ever. The ink on these pages has been a doorway through which my family has relived each moment shared here. I am so grateful to capture these lessons so that we can continue to learn from them in the future.

So many people worked behind the scenes to make this book a reality. Thank you, Jack Countryman, for introducing me to the Zondervan team. Thank you, Andy Rogers, for seeing the value of this story and for taking a chance on an unknown author. Thank you, Dirk Buursma, for being the guardian of my ideas during the editing process. Your encouragements greatly enhanced these pages. Amanda Halash, Caitlin Vander Meulen, and David Morris, your editorial and administrative contributions are second to none! Thank you, Kait Lamphere, for working so hard to make each page visually pleasant. Thank you, Curt Diepenhorst, for producing a beautiful cover. Finally, I'm grateful to Brandon Henderson and Trinity McFadden for your efforts to spread the word about this hidden treasure.

To our St. Jude family, thank you for providing first-class

care for my son. Walking the halls of your hospital has forever changed who I am. My family will remain with you in the fight against childhood cancer.

To my brother, William Dooley, thank you for being the first eyes to read my work. Your insights and guidance have been priceless.

To the saints at Sunnyvale First Baptist Church, thank you for encouraging me to write and for giving me the time to do so.

To the saints at Englewood Baptist Church, I love being your pastor. I pray these words will encourage and strengthen your faith.

To my kids, being your dad is my greatest accomplishment. Thank you for giving me time away to write.

To my wife, Heather, you are my rock. Our journey has not been easy, nor has it been everything we expected, but I would not trade one moment of walking with you by my side. God knows every sacrifice you have made for our family. Thank you for encouraging me to complete this manuscript. I love you.

To Jesus, every day with You grows sweeter. Thank You for loving me and patiently transforming me. I pray that You will continue to glorify Yourself through our family.